POLITICAL AUTHORITY AND MORAL JUDGMENT

POLITICAL AUTHORITY
AND MORAL JUDGMENT

GLENN NEGLEY

DUKE UNIVERSITY PRESS
Durham, North Carolina
1 9 6 5

© 1965, Duke University Press

Library of Congress Catalogue Card number 65-13654

PRINTED IN THE UNITED STATES OF AMERICA
BY HERITAGE PRINTERS, INC., CHARLOTTE, N. C.

To

JULIA

Man's best possession is a sympathetic wife.

—Euripides

ACKNOWLEDGMENTS

Much of the research which was a major stimulus to this work was made possible by a grant from the Ford Foundation which enabled me to spend a year in Europe, mainly in Vienna during the four-power occupation. The generosity and latitude of this assistance permitted work and observation from which I still profit.

The warmth of my acknowledgment to The Administrative Staff College, Henley-on-Thames, England, is a reflection of the hospitality which I experienced there. For Sir Noel Hall (then Principal of the College, now Master of Brasenose College), my gratitude encompasses both fruitful relationship and friendly regard.

It is perhaps somewhat unusual to thank the anonymous "readers" who editorially appraise a manuscript; I should like to express to them, whoever they may be, my sincere appreciation for their judicious and helpful comments.

The opportunity provided by editors of the following publications to publish preliminary excursions into some of the subjects of this work was of great benefit: *Ethics; Utah Law Review; Freedom and Authority; Symbols and Values.*

The University Council on Research, Duke University, has provided continued assistance for research, writing, and publication; their encouraging support has, in a very real sense, made this and other work possible.

GLENN NEGLEY

Durham, North Carolina
7 July 1964

CONTENTS

POLITICAL AUTHORITY AND MORAL JUDGMENT

POLITICAL AUTHORITY

Difficulties concerning the meaning of "authority" alone, and the effort to define that in terms of acceptance of an obligation to obey, merely raise many problems which could probably be solved in good measure by precise analysis which recognized that law is an essential component of the political process, and included careful efforts to distinguish law from other norms.[1]

THE sharpest conflicts of political opposition arise when the subject of debate is law. It is odd that strife should be engendered over the very symbol of order, justice, and equity; the apparent oddity leads men to reject what they hopefully hold must be a paradox, and to proclaim wishfully that in respect to the fundamental rightness of "law" men *must* agree. The wish is pious but contrary to fact, and no degree of fervor in proclamation will fulfil it.

If, of course, the term "law" is used so distributively as to indicate merely that all organizations of men in social polities have laws, the observation is correct but relatively trivial. One might also affirm the truism that all social organizations have members, but specification requires that these members be severally described as ants, birds, rats, or men; if men, they may be wise or stupid, tolerant or bigoted, merciful or ruthless. So, while law is a definitive characteristic of all political societies, it is not enlightening to insist that therefore all men "agree" on law, for this is very much like saying that men, with rare and unusual exceptions, agree to eat and sleep.

1. Jerome Hall, "Unification of Political and Legal Theory," *Political Science Quarterly*, LXIX (1954), 18.

When law is given specifiable and evaluative content (meaning that in this less than ideal world methodological and valuational alternatives will be unavoidable), then disagreement arises and sharpens. Which law is best, preferable, good, or just—and why? The framework of communication in this controversy is complicated, tortuous, and obscure. Indeed, the purpose here is to attempt some small clarification of what it is we are talking about when we disagree as to which law is "best," whether the disagreement be between men or between states.

The discussion to follow will draw heavily on the historical development of the discrimination of law from other kinds of authority; it is indicative of the climate of opinion in our time that one almost feels constrained to apologize for suggesting that the philosophers and jurists who have concerned themselves with this problem might have said something worth attending to even though they were not primarily interested in the semantics of the controversy. Certain parallel citations will suggest that we have during the past hundred years or so added very little to the clarification of this problem of legal authority. Indeed, if nothing more is accomplished here than to point out some of the contributions to the clarification of the facts of political authority, and perhaps to note implications for further thought, the achievement will be satisfactory.

The temper of our times suggests also an observation or two about the intent of a philosophical inquiry into the nature of political authority. Never before has the attention of men been so concentrated on the achievement of orderly relations between nations, for in our world it is manifest that all degrees of internal and domestic harmony depend critically and precariously on the maintenance of peaceful and legal external relations. It is redundant to remark that calculations based on the imminent destruction of mankind and civilization would make a discussion of political and legal authority somewhat less than sensible. Therefore, it is necessary to presume that mankind is not going to destroy itself; while some of those now suffering nuclear neurosis may find this a questionably optimistic assumption, there seems some justification for the premise.

We could, of course, resolve the problem of authority by eliminating ourselves, but this seems a remote possibility. If we make an exception of that extraordinary little animal, the lemming, it is doubtful that there has ever existed a creature that has tried as systematically and ingeniously to exterminate itself as has man. His lack of success in this bizarre endeavor may induce in some a faith in supernatural providence; at least it should, on historical grounds, deter us from an expectation of man's predictable demise. There is certainly no intention here of trying to trivialize a serious consideration, but it seems meaningful to ask whether we evidence a tendency to overstate the peculiarity, and especially the unresolvable nature, of the problems presented by the development of so-called atomic weapons. Men have been hurling missiles of some kind at one another for a long time, and their children's children have suffered from the diseases and ravages of war; it is questionable whether the prospect of imminent devastation can be relevant to philosophical discourse.

It would be a most unrealistic philosopher who could be unmindful of the potential of today's weapons for horror, death, and destruction; but some historical perspective might serve to focus our attention on the thought that in the history of modern warfare no state has suffered the fate of Carthage. During the devastating wars of recent times, the populations of the warring states have increased, and their economies, like the birth rate, have seemed to acquire impetus from what ought to be ruinous destruction. However grisly the contemplation, we might proceed more objectively with the reminder that if we should somehow manage to kill five out of six persons in the world next year—an almost inconceivable accomplishment even for modern weapons, the population of the world would still be as large as it was when John Locke wrote his *Letters on Tolerance* and Pufendorf his *Elements of Uni-*

versal Jurisprudence. The problem of political authority and legal order would remain the most profound and the most critical of man's practical concerns. Let us proceed, therefore, as if the method of reduction by radiation is not a realistic alternative to the effort to resolve the problems of social order by rational processes. An adequate consideration of the concept and fact of authority cannot be dissociated from value discriminations, and unless we are prepared to accept a fantastically arbitrary abridgment of values to one monolithic pattern, there is a sense in which we must admit that different kinds of authority are distinguished by the values they purport to authorize. Endeavor will be made to avoid the overzealous semantic and linguistic quibbling that becomes so introspectively subjective as to mistake word-mongering for factual analysis. On the other hand, it is an elementary requirement of sensible discourse that we try to be as clear as possible in respect to the factual referents of our language. There are describable alternatives of reference for the concept of authority, and meaningful discussion can proceed only if we are reasonably clear as to which of these alternatives we are talking about. If we are blending into a confused admixture different meanings of authority, the difference of definitive framework will make communication difficult and meaning unsubstantial. The most unresolvable kind of confusion will occur when observable factual political authority is supported by reference to a value assertion which is irrelevant or inappropriate to that kind of authority.

At the outset, there is a fundamental, even primitive, definitive distinction that must be observed if our examination of legal controversy is not to be hopelessly muddled from the very start by confusion as to what the words we are using *mean.* It is extraordinarily difficult to unravel a confusion that has become embalmed in usage, for the references of ordinary discourse find their way even into our more deliberative diction. Yet, at a very basic level of discrimination, we must note carefully the ambiguities of the term *rule* as descriptive of patterns regulating behavior. The regulation of behavior may or may not involve reference to authority; if authority is invoked, it may or may not be legal or political authority. Perhaps this is an emphasis of the obvious, but it is precisely in the neglect of the obvious that the question of legal authority begins to be muddled. Within the context of legal and political authority, we find that *rule* is used to refer to two quite different things, and unless this difference of reference is noted, it is likely that a meaning will be imported into the use of *rule* that makes little sense in terms of factual reference.

One use of *rule* refers to an act or circumstance in which forceful control is exerted over a specifiable area of action; in this sense, *rule* is properly used as "the rule of Henry VIII," "a rule of the Court," or the "rule of the Interstate Commerce Commission." As so used, *rule* is approximately equivalent to "prevailing authority."

A second way in which *rule* can properly be used is to refer to certain operational procedures, generally rather arbitrary, which are designed and accepted in order to facilitate the prosecution of a certain purpose. In this reference, we speak of "Robert's rules of order," the "rules" of etiquette, and the "rules" of bridge or baseball or hopscotch.[2]

2. These are the two meanings of *rule* which are pertinent to our discussion here, in which we are concerned with the use of *rule* as implying legal or political authority. However, it is important to note that in the extensive and sometimes vague use of the term *rule* it is mandatory for the sake of sense to distinguish as clearly as possible what kind of authority is being imputed to the term as used. It is by no means easy to discriminate the authority-reference of such widely used expressions as the Golden Rule, the rule of thumb, the rule of three. The term *rule* has a range of meaning, especially in respect to the dominant concept of authority implicit in the particular use, which is a challenge to the most perspicacious examination; only confusion can result from the random use of this somewhat insidious term.

When, for example, H. L. A. Hart (in his introduction to a new edition of Austin's *The Province of Jurisprudence Determined* [New York, 1954]) suggests, with the air of making a profound observation, that "if Austin's doctrine were to be amended by the introduction of the notion of a rule at the appropriate points, many of its separate faults would disappear," one reads on, eagerly awaiting Professor Hart's definition of what he means by *rule*, for the sense of the statement depends on this clarification. However, in the eighteen pages of his introduction, this essential definition is not forthcoming. We are thus left with an observation that is not meaningful, since Professor Hart gives us the option of assuming that he meant Austin should have introduced into his doc-

An apparent obsession with the concept of *rule* has characterized some recent theorizing about political and legal authority. It is argued that what is meant by legal order is the
acceptance of rules in internal and external relations, not very
illuminating rhetoric unless there is some specification of
what is meant by *rule*. Such statements are more productive
of confusion than clarification, since they employ as synonymous concepts which can and do have quite different meanings. We may or may not be reasonably clear about what we
mean by *law;* we are certainly very indefinite about what constitutes a *rule* in this context. There is, for example, much
talk about the "Rule of Law," but very little specification of
what this means, or could mean. Instead of trying to specify
and distinguish these concepts, and thereby give them a proper
meaning in respect to authority, we are more likely to import
into them surreptitiously an intent and a value connotation
which cannot be justified by a verbal symbol, however hopeful
and pious its utterance.

We use the terms *rule* and *law* as if they were synonymous,
or at least as if the reference were to the same kind of thing,
and we have been encouraged in this linguistic reduction by
the careless analysis of some recent philosophical work. The
distinction is a rather elementary one, and the extended notice
of it here might be ill-considered were it not for the widespread
and somewhat dogmatic conclusions that are now being derived from this misuse of the concept of *rule*. In respect to
the regulation of political and legal behavior, the term *rule*
has two quite different references, and hence two distinguishable meanings. The first refers to some kind of existing control by authority; the second meaning refers to operations
which derive their force only from the continued agreement,
on the part of those participating in the action surveyed, to
use such operations. If the contexts of the two references are

---

trine the notion of the rule of Queen Victoria, the Golden Rule, the rule of
thumb, or indeed the rules of cricket. (Cf. the comment of Alan Gewirth in a
review of this reprint: *Ethics*, LXVII [1957], 222.)

confused, and if the meaning of the first reference is imparted into a use in the second sense, a complete misinterpretation of the factual situation will ensue. An even worse distortion results if the authoritative connotation of the first meaning is reduced to the pragmatic arbitrariness of the second.

In the first sense of *rule,* that in which there is a reference to authority, there is a certain equivalence to what we generally mean by the term *law,* for *law* seems to mean "prevailing authority." However, the use of *rule* as synonymous with *law,* together with careless lack of discrimination between the two distinguishable references of *rule,* has resulted in some rather disturbing ambiguities. These ambiguities lead to serious confusion of facts and norms, with a resultant muddle of the entire problem of authority and value. A notable example of this kind of simplified confusion is provided by T. D. Weldon:

> There are important differences between politics and games but the function of rules in both of them is the same. There is no point in attempting to distinguish between the laws of England and the laws of croquet from this point of view.[3]

Weldon admits that it is probably advisable to "solemnize" the law, since it appears somewhat more serious to break the "law" than to infringe the "by-laws of the local golf-club." The difference, however, is merely one of degree.

> Rules as we have already seen are prescriptions. . . . We make them up. We do not find or discover them except in the sense that we read them in books or legal codes. We may guess what the rules of England or the rules of cricket are by observing the behaviour of Englishmen and cricketers.[4]

It is interesting to note how Weldon attempts to support this reduction of state law to rules of the game, for he typifies the contortion of fact necessary to support the semantic construction. There is something fascinating about the stubborn belief that artificially contrived verbal simplicity can be im-

3. *The Vocabulary of Politics* (Baltimore: Penguin Books, 1955), p. 67.
4. *Ibid.,* p. 191.

posed upon fact, thereby reducing an intrinsically complex factual situation to a factually simple one. The idealists at least tried to support their impositions on the external world by appeal to metaphysics, and this seems altogether more reputable than the pomposity of belligerent assertion. To the argument that there is an essential difference between the laws of a state and the rules of a cricket club, since the status of the individual in respect to these two kinds of authority is quite different, Weldon replies:

> At most there is a difference of degree, and even this is difficult to establish at all firmly. . . . But to say that one cannot escape from one's State is simply untrue. Normally emigration is possible, though it is sometimes so difficult as to be practically out of the question. But there is always suicide, and it is not in these days so very uncommon.[5]

So is accomplished a complete reduction or evasion of the critical problem cited by Hall: "to distinguish laws from other norms." The establishment of an equivalence between resignation from a club because of disagreement with a rule that shorts may not be worn in the dining room, and the taking of one's own life because one cannot morally countenance the directives of the law of the state and yet cannot otherwise escape its authority—this would engender such a confusion of norms as to make quite impossible any "precise analysis which recognized that law is an essential component of the political process."[6]

The problem of value discrimination cannot, however, be evaded; as Weldon himself admits, "We cannot avoid taking sides." On what basis, then, do we "take sides" in accepting or rejecting authority? It seems not to be quite so arbitrary and whimsical as the acceptance or rejection of rules. Weldon suggests:

> Each of us has his own tests, which are no doubt rough and crude, but they will serve their purpose, which is to

5. *Ibid.*, pp. 48-49.
6. Hall, *loc. cit.* For a suggestion of what actually is involved in the tragic situation in which the law presents to the individual only the alternatives of value denial or suicide, see below, pp. 133, 136-7.

check and confirm the conclusions of experts based on thorough research.[7]

It is somewhat novel to argue that one can confirm his acceptance of authority by reference to the "conclusions of experts." Weldon's criteria, on this basis, are interesting:

1. Does the political system under consideration censor the reading of those who are subject to it and impose restrictions on teaching?
2. Does it maintain that any political or other principles are immutable and therefore beyond criticism?
3. Does it impose restrictions on the intercourse of its members with those who live under different systems?
   . . . Any set of institutions which includes all these restrictions is *prima facie* a bad one.[8]

The language here is very loose and unprecise; it is readily apparent that the restrictions formulated by Weldon are, in the form of rules, common to a wide range of voluntary organizations, such as religious, fraternal, even business and educational institutions. Membership in any institution imposes certain restrictions on the individual; discrimination as to whether such restrictions are or are not "bad" is not a matter of *prima facie* evidence.[9] In support of the *prima facie* badness of such restrictions, Weldon returns to the misleading identification of *rule* and *law*: "The reason for claiming that it [a set of institutions] is bad is the presumption that those who are subject to it would reject it or escape from it if the restrictions were removed."[10]

This purported empirical test will not survive empirical application; such restrictions are frequently and voluntarily accepted by individuals for the sake of membership in the institution which imposes the restrictions. Weldon must admit, hence, that what he presents is not a "test" at all, but rather a "personal view, or prejudice if that word is preferred. It has

7. *Op. cit.*, pp. 175-176.
8. *Ibid.*, p. 176.
9. See, for example, W. H. Whyte, Jr., *The Organization Man* (New York, 1957).
10. *Op. cit.*, p. 176.

nothing philosophical about it and may be rejected by anyone
who disapproves of it."[11] We have here, then, an "I like" assertion; how quickly the non-rational becomes the irrational is
evidenced when Weldon adds a summary judgment to his
three "tests":

    4. Do the rulers of the association which has these institu-
       tions find most of their supporters among the illiterate,
       the uneducated, and the superstitious?[12]

This kind of easy and casual analysis of the problem of authority and value has lured many down a primrose path of delu-
sion. It *is* easy to presume that those who accept any authority,
any restrictions which we ourselves would not accept, are
doing so because of ignorance, stupidity, or superstition. It is
simply incredible that all persons, had they free choice, would
not elect our "way of life"! Yet the fact is that they sometimes
do not; not all men turn upon my "path of righteousness."

    The assumption that the laws of a state are equivalent to
rules, and that these can be abridged or rejected on the basis
of mere personal preference, leads to some very abortive mis-
calculations. Law carries an authority which rules of a game
do not manifest; there is a factual distinction between the two,
and that distinction must be maintained if there is to be any
clarity or sense in our political and legal discourse. Even in
ordinary discourse, where we are likely to use *law* and *rule*
with a careless kind of equivalence, we would consider it very
odd—and incorrect—to talk about the "laws of bridge," the
"laws of etiquette," or the "laws of cricket." The authority of
law involves something more than mere arbitrary and voluntary acceptance, although this may be one element in the complex of legal authority. The complicated problem of what constitutes authority in a political complex cannot be resolved
by reference to the preferential and arbitrary. We must recognize the implication that law implies an authority different
from that of mere rule, and try to understand the source and

11. *Ibid.*
12. *Ibid.*

ground of that authority. Otherwise, we shall not be able to answer sensibly the question of what law is even possible, much less what law is best.

The concept of authority has become almost meaningless in legal and political theory. It seems unnecessary to argue that law must have authority. That those rules which can properly be designated *law* do manifest and exert authority also seems clear—else there would be no law, by definition. But what it is that contributes authority to a given law—and not to every axiom—does not seem clear from an examination of legal and juristic speculation. Throughout history, law has laid claim to final authority in ordering the mundane relations of men in social organization; law has admitted itself to be the highest achievement of rationality in secular affairs; law has magnanimously offered itself to man as the only hope of order and peace in society. Yet, at the very moment when men need principles of order in social organization more critically than ever in history, those who tell us *what* the law is cannot tell us *why* it is law. Thus law presents the hazard of a richly ornamented structure resting precariously on a foundation which fluctuates with every tidal wave of history. The law can but follow the inclinations and dictates of a source of power itself quite external to, and independent of, the law. The law can offer its formal system as a language that has in the past served more or less usefully to communicate the dictates of many authorities, but the services proffered by law will have to prove themselves amenable to the purposes and ends of the external authority. Laws made do not even slow down dictators in the making.

The many sources which historically have been exploited as grounds for the authority of law have uniformly failed to provide adequate factual substantiation of their claims. Consequently, many of those interested in the theory and practice of law seem now to accept the fact that law is indeed nothing more than a necessary and useful instrument for communicating the social purposes of prevailing monopolies of power. The jurist thus becomes in the eyes of his professional colleagues a kind of social mathematician who employs his system and his skill with a cultivated disregard of everything but the formal mechanics of his manipulations. In this manner the law achieves an apparent objectivity which releases it from all concern for value considerations, as well as from the troublesome task of accounting for and justifying the authority which enforces the law. In most cases, the authority which dictates the law is referred to as "political"; but this is certainly mere wishful thinking on the part of the jurist, for he knows very well that the political is but one of many forms of power monopoly. If the law is, in fact, simply a tool and instrument of the authority emanating from a prevailing monopoly of power, then it must surely be admitted that law will have to acquiesce in the demands of *any* authority which wields a monopoly of power—and that will not necessarily be the political. Perhaps the most vicious of the forms of power to which law will in such circumstances find itself subservient is that of sheer power, unqualified and undisciplined force. The submission of law to force is a complete *reductio* of law and legal process.

While unquestionably many now engaged in legal speculation do not accept the cynical relativist description of law, this position has rather clearly marked the recent development of law as it functions in social organization. It is fashionable now to deprecate reason and logic, and references to value are distinctly old-fashioned. It is considered smarter to exorcise the problems of reason and value in the law by attaching the symbols of Freudian psychology, economic class struggle, or political power to legislation and the judicial process. The substitution of name-attachment for rational analysis is not a tendency confined to our own day. These new symbols no more clarify the problem of legal authority than did the symbol of sovereignty, and Pound was quite right when he remarked, "It is a boast rather than a description to call such teaching 'realism.' "[13] Realism, if it means anything in law or elsewhere,

13. Roscoe Pound, *Social Control through Law* (New Haven, 1942), p. 97.

is characterized by reference to and rational analysis of *fact*.

It may be that the relativist description of law is correct, and that there simply are no facts to support a non-relativistic position. It may be that right and wrong, good and bad, true and false, as well as legal and illegal, cannot be properly distinguished except by reference to economic perspective, power blocs, or maladjusted sex life. It may be; but those who present these arguments have not yet shown this to be the case. To be sure, the maintenance of objectivity in analysis is the most difficult task of reason, and it is always valuable and useful to have pointed out all instances in which objectivity has not been observed, if the causes of non-objectivity can be described and corrected. In this respect, the descriptive methods above mentioned could have a beneficial effect on the legal process, in the same manner in which Bentham and Austin had a most beneficial effect by calling attention to the fact that law should be precisely formulated and widely publicized. Yet, before we rush to join in the riotous abandonment of reason, to frolic in libido unveilings and the unconstrained manipulation of power blocs, reason ought to be given a chance. There is a considerable amount of evidence to support the claim that reason in law has brought man well along the way toward civilization—though not very speedily. It is certainly premature to abandon reason as a failure.

Men of ulterior motivation and sinister purpose have always deprecated the use of reason, appealing rather to the vigorous efficacy of will, and the struggle against apostles of power unrestrained by reason is a continuing one. The peculiar despair of our own period, however, arises from the spectacle of reasonable men of good intention forced to an abandonment of reason in affairs political and legal—a tragedy of philosophy, not of diplomacy or procedures or practice. If blame is to accrue for the awkwardness of legal states in maneuvering against the forceful thrust of police monopolies, if the recital of vague sentimentalities of moral conviction substitutes poorly for critically needed intellectual support in the dogged effort to establish legal procedures among states, the guilt is obvious. It is a sad commentary indeed that legal theory must yet refer for rational and philosophical substantiation to philosophers of the nineteenth century—if not indeed to Aristotle. It is sadder still that lapse of time should have dulled the point of their speculation in the casuistry of academic exegesis.

Nothing is easier than to seek out ways of leveling devastating criticism at the instances of rational analysis which have contributed to the structure of law as it has developed historically. The analysis of fact is a slow and sometimes painfully tortuous process. One of the characteristics which distinguishes the development of science, so-called, from the history of more speculative enterprises is the respect manifested by the scientist for those who laid the foundations upon which alone his analysis is possible. In law and philosophy, however, there is a minimum of recognition of the progressive collaboration of knowledge. Philosophers tend either to become Kantians or to feel the necessity of proving everything Kantian to be wrong, and many legal theorists manifest the same susceptibility to the lures of a "system." Of American jurists, none has evidenced a greater appreciation and understanding of the historical development of the law than Pound. His erudite acquaintance with and respect for the historical development of law as the principle of order in social relations furnished a proper ground for his analysis of the present task of law. His recognition of the influence of philosophic thought on the legal tradition, as well as of the philosophical nature of the further development of the theory of law, was more profound and productive than the attitude of those whose major criticism seems to be that Pound did not adopt the particular set of symbols which they are using as a substitute for reason.

In a series of lectures which constitute a kind of summary statement of his philosophy of law, Pound expressed concern at the defeatist attitude of current legal relativism. His words should weigh heavily on those who wish to see power controlled under law:

If we give up what we have sought to do in the past and say let those who control the force of politically organized society make such threats as seem good to them, either upon such reasons as appeal to them or without reasons, we give up what has made law a prime agency of civilization since the days of the classical Roman jurists.[14]

Pound objected to the abandonment of law and civilization to the forces of the irrational and the illegal. Law still has a proper function to perform in society:

Is it not a real problem, something more than a pious wish, to find how to recognize the claims of A and those of B without destroying either—and without leaving it to A and B to seek a solution by trying each to destroy the other?[15]

Here is realism which sees clearly the task of law in society, not the pusillanimous abandonment of law because its efforts fall short of absolute universality and eternal validity.

Law is a practical matter. If we cannot establish a demonstrated universal legal measure of values which everyone will agree to, it does not follow that we must give up and turn society over to unchecked force.[16]

Such a philosophy of law, to which no reasonable person can take exception, defines law as a rational process of achieving order in society. A rational process is distinguished from revelation and other miracle-working by the gradual development of its results. There is a very muddled kind of thinking in the assumption that the only alternative to dogmatism, in law or elsewhere, is a relapse into unperceptive relativism; to hold a result as tentative to the further development of the rational process of analysis is not thereby to forego all criteria. On the other hand, it is equally absurd to grasp dogma as the only salvation from unsatisfactory relativism. Weakness of intellect is betrayed in both escapes.[17]

14. *Ibid.*
15. *Ibid.*, p. 101.
16. *Ibid.*, p. 108.
17. In contrast to such counsels of despair, see the sensible and informed analysis of Charles Frankel: *The Case for Modern Man* (New York, 1956).

Pound and a few others like him have continued to empha-
size the necessity of philosophical analysis to the development
of legal theory. That they have held to this opinion despite
the almost total lack of concern or competence evidenced by
professional philosophers indicates that legal speculation is
fast becoming the final repository of all interest and ability in
what could properly be called political philosophy. The tremendous influence on—one might almost say the direction of
—the historical development of law by philosophy is a matter
of record. It is not therefore surprising that philosophers' neglect of the practical and theoretical problems adduced by law
should result in an increasing tendency on the part of legal
theory to fall back upon relativism as the only alternative to
dogmas proved inadequate. Not often will philosophy provide
law with the stimulus of a Hegel or a Bentham; but Pound was
properly disdainful of those philosophers who would give up
reason to disillusionment unless they are promised omni-
science.

The problem of the authority of law is but one of many
which beg the clarification that comes only from many efforts
to seek out and describe the pertinent facts. Perhaps it is more
nearly correct to say that the problem of authority marks one
of many directions of analysis, one perspective toward the pertinent body of fact. However this may appear, the question of
the legal imperative is one which will always demand attention
in any definition or description of law. The problem is particularly pertinent at this time because the question of authority
has been neglected for so long, while other developments in
law have gone on, that it now seems impossible for legal speculation to make even a gesture of rationality toward defining
the imperative of law. So Pound, for all his understanding of
the fundamental issues of current legal theory, reneged on the
question: "What is the source of authority of the legal
order?"[18] After indicating that current legal thought on the
question is not illuminating, Pound rested his case on faith.

18. *Op. cit.,* p. 51.

> But the legal order goes on, whatever may be the basis of whatever rightful authority it has, and I submit it has kept and holds an actual authority because it performs, and performs well, its task of reconciling and harmonizing conflicting and overlapping human demands and so maintains a social order in which we may maintain and further civilization.[19]

This is piety of a very high order indeed, but it neatly sidesteps the problem which recent and current events so forcefully formulate for us: *Is* there any "rightful authority" to which a legal order can appeal when the very existence of legal order is attacked by an authority which is not "legally rightful"? The justification of such authority, it would appear, is the only suitable answer to the skeptical relativists against whom Pound inveighed. Faith without facts is an unpromising antagonist of force; the maintenance of legal order depends upon the establishment of a rational ground of legal authority, the most critical practical demand upon philosophy today; the endeavor must be so encompassing that every effort in this direction serves a useful purpose.

The police state, properly so called, is not concerned with the justification of its administration in terms of any system of values. The legal state, if it is properly so designated, must be obligated to justify its acts on grounds of value discrimination. That the morally right does not possess political might is axiomatic; but if the relation of legal authority and value significance is to remain a paradoxical surd in our thinking, then indeed the structure of social organization must be relinquished to the protagonists of undisciplined will—and the abandonment of reason is complete. Perhaps the concept of rule will prove helpful and necessary in the assessment of the relation of authority and value; the prospect for legal order is, however, very dim if we rely upon men and states to abide by the "rules of the game."

19. *Ibid.*, pp. 53-54.

CHAPTER II

AUTHORITY AS
LEGAL IMPERATIVE

Traditionally the most common basis of obedience is no reason at all—not to raise the awkward question: to assume obedience, as the parent, associating obedience with affection and protection, superiority, and perhaps a little pressure of force. So the fatherhood of power was simple, and the rule of the elders almost as simple. Magic and the club were at hand to quicken the sluggish imagination or silence the querulous tongue, raised like that of Thersites. But in time the ideologies of power appeared and began their century-long struggle for survival.[1]

DEFINITION of facts and terms is the prerequisite of rational discourse. In the case of law, however, definition cannot be accomplished by the comparatively easy linear process of classification. The subject of inquiry in legal theory is in great measure the determination of precisely what constitutes law. Whether there is a corresponding objectivity in fact to which law refers, whether there is some principle in the ordering of action which can properly be designated law—these are not mere matters of observation at the empirical level. Accepted procedures of empirical observation have not yet defined law within the limits of descriptive judgment. The gratuitous assumption that law has an objective, factual status, but can be descriptively defined only by some non-rational, private method of observation, is a contradiction in terms and an affront to intelligent analysis and appraisal. Rational analy-

---

1. Charles E. Merriam, *Systematic Politics* (Chicago, 1945), p. 96.

sis of law must then proceed through the use of admittedly hypothetical definitions. With this understanding, let us examine what appears to be the essential nature of law.

In the first place, despite the present bad odor of Austinian theory, it is nevertheless the case that law must be a command.[2] The imperative element of law is its most fundamental and important characteristic; without the command which promises punishment for disobedience, the most just, the most moral, the most equitable, the most hopeful formulation becomes an embarrassment. There is hardly anything more absurd than a statement which commands, but which cannot *demand* obedience by the execution of punishment. Bentham and Austin were quite correct in defining law as essentially imperative in nature, but the concept of command which satisfied Austin was so shallow and artless that it very shortly suffered the depreciation it deserved. Unfortunately, the inadequacy of Austin's description diverted attention from the important clarification of what actually *does* constitute the imperative element of law other than the simple and erroneous relation of "superior and inferior" which Austin assumed it to be. Too many theorists have indulged in the illusion that an exposition of the inadequacy of the Imperative Theory is a solution of the theory of the imperative.

Some of the reaction to Austinian jurisprudence has indeed been so uncritical as deliberately to direct attention away from the crucial problem of the legal imperative. Thus, Robson contends: "Much confusion both in jurisprudence and in

2. We must not be distracted from a reasonable course of investigation by unreasonable semantic or theoretic quibbling. It is a captivating temptation to believe that one is saying something new when coining a new word for an old concept. The word "command" is a sensible expression which can be given some definiteness of meaning; it is used here as the term best expressing the meaning intended. If "command" implies an ineradicable Austinian connotation for the reader, let him substitute another term of his own choice, rather than thrust the argument into the worn pigeon-hole of "command theory of jurisprudence."

"It has become commonplace to criticize Austin severely, to deplore his influence, and to treat him as made of the same cloth as are 20th-century positivists. I believe much of this criticism is fallacious and that until careful reappraisals of Austin are attempted, important issues of contemporary jurisprudence will remain clouded" (Jerome Hall, "Reason and Reality in Jurisprudence," *Buffalo Law Review,* VII [1958], 357).

science results, I believe, from the false importance given to the ideas of 'command' and 'obedience' in connection with law."[3] It would indeed be an oversimplification of a rather elementary kind to define law merely in terms of "command" and "obedience"; but this is quite a different thing from the recognition of the imperative as an essential ingredient of legal formulation and execution. It may be true, as Robson contends, that "English legal thought since Bentham has run in narrow grooves";[4] yet it might be argued that this narrowness of development is, at least in part, the result of unperceptive interpretation.[5] The concept of command is given a peculiarly limited definition when it is asserted:

> It is impossible to co-operate in any field of endeavor without agreeing to submit to a common rule of conduct; and sanctions need not necessarily play any part at all in such an agreement. It is absurd to pretend that an English merchant in the 17th century was not bound to abide by the rules of the law merchant until Lord Mansfield had told him that he was so bound.[6]

Here again we encounter an ambiguous use of the concept of "rule," and even more open to latitude of description is the reference to "sanctions." One may be "sanctioned" out of a game of bridge if he refuses to abide by the agreed-upon rules; the merchant might have been sanctioned out of economic activity for failure to observe the accepted rules. Rule in this sense certainly implies sanction, if only the minimal sanction imposed by agreement. Surely the term "rule" cannot be used sensibly without an implication of some kind of sanction. It is not a question of whether or not the rule is enforced by sanction; the question is as to the nature of the enforcing sanction. The manner in which the merchant was bound by the sanction of his fellow merchants, and the nature of his status as bound by legal judicial decision, are decidedly and factually different

3. William A. Robson, *Civilization and the Growth of Law* (New York, 1935), p. 292.
4. *Ibid.*, p. 254.
5. See below, chap. iv.
6. Robson, *op. cit.*, p. 298.

in kind. In the first instance, he might well have been excluded from the "game" of merchant activity; in the second case, he is subject to penalties which the law may impose and enforce, up to and including the deprivation, not only of property, but of life and liberty. Why Lord Mansfield considered it reasonable, feasible, or necessary to add the full weight of legal sanction to the existing economic sanction is quite another matter. One might indeed refer to each of these instances of the use of sanctions as the application of a "rule," but the difference in the factual nature of the sanctions employed indicates precisely the distinction which must be maintained between "common rules of conduct" and what may properly be designated law.

It was precisely in the statement of command and sanction as elementary concepts in the definition of law that Bentham posed the problem of the imperative. It is true that he did not develop that suggestion, at least not in any of his published works. That this promising direction of thought has not been pursued since Bentham's day is a result, at least in part, of failure to comprehend the essential nature of sanctions as the source of the authority of law. Bentham described four general types of sanction: physical, moral, religious, and political. Of these, he eliminated the physical as not a proper legal sanction. The stimulation of Bentham's exploration lies in the possibility that he was suggesting the institutional nature of the fundamental sanctions of law, a description extraordinarily different from the vain effort to discover an imperative in codified statute or judicial dictum.[7]

A legal imperative can be defined as that factual configuration which supports and endorses the command of law as execution in action. Lest this appear a simple tautology, it must be remembered that an imperative is not constituted by the manner of statement thereof. A law is not constructed merely by submitting a wish or a desire to legalistic formulation. Not every statement which commands "Thou shalt" or "Thou

7. For a further discussion of Bentham's views, see chap. iv below.

shalt not" is such as to demand and elicit obedience. What then shall we say of a command that does not in fact command? There is little that we can say except that a command which does not *in fact* command is not *in fact* a command. Nor can we allow that a law, which claims imperativeness as an essential element of its definition, be granted the status of law in fact unless it evidences an imperative in fact—unless, in short, it commands *action*.

This reasonable demand, that a law which is not in fact a law be called something other than law, does not simplify the task of defining law. But the confusion is considerably less than that which results when the distinction is neglected, for it allows us at the outset to disencumber our analysis from a vast amount of pseudo-legal formulation which has hopefully, and sometimes dramatically and aggressively, laid claim to the legal imperative. Failure to detect that the ground for these claims was allegorical rather than factual tended in many cases to divert the attention of legal speculation from the proper factual analysis of law to exclusive concern with the elaboration and celebration of the allegory.

The imperative of law to which reference is made here is not therefore simply the imperative of grammatical form. Linguistic structures are indeed important, and primary and troublesome confusion in any subject cannot be avoided unless a careful distinction is maintained between semantic analysis and factual analysis. Nothing is more patent than that the absence of clarity and precision in the statement of law will nullify whatever force and effectiveness it might otherwise have had. However, had it not a force and effectiveness distinguishable from and antecedent to its semantic construction, it would hardly derive them from linguistic symbols, however clear and precise. To be sure, there are those in recent years who would limit analysis to linguistic juxtaposition; for them, the imperative of law follows from the manufacture and formulation of linguistic symbols. For them, there is no *legal* imperative. The restriction of analysis to the level of semantic formulation has introduced confusion, not only in respect to the factual issues in question, but also in regard to the proper function and relation of semantic analysis itself.[8]

We cannot, therefore, accept as other than rhetoric the kind of evasion which tries to avoid the problem of the imperative by asserting that the law is what the judges say it is, that it is what the courts declare, or that it is what is done officially. There is, for example, the point of view typically expressed by John Dickinson: "Whatever forces can be said to influence the growth of the law they exert that influence only by in-fluencing the judges."[9] To this Cardozo would add that there will be as many estimates of those forces as there are judges on the bench. In a companion article to that by Dickinson, Dean Leon Green states the same view in slightly different language: "Insofar as the sources of law are apparent, they are found in the judgments of the individuals who are entrusted with the power to pass these judgments."[10] We can certainly agree with Green that authority is not to be found in the language of the law, and we might also agree with his assertion that the judge is the most responsible individual in society because it is his judgment which proclaims law. But proclamation does not constitute law. When two judges, or ten judges, of equal re-sponsibility proclaim incompatible judgments as to what con-stitutes the law in a given instance, then what is the law? It is neither impertinent nor trivial to ask this question. It would but continue the circle of evasion at a more naïve level to answer that the judgment of the court of highest appeal will constitute the law. All courts can err in their proclamation of law, because all men can err in judgment. Err about what— other than the nature and source of that authority which they assume will contribute the necessary element of imperation to their proclamation? Without that imperative, their proclama-

8. As a case in point, see the pertinent comments of James Ward Smith (*Theme for Reason* [Princeton, 1957], pp. 164-166) on the definition by Herbert Feigl of a rule of procedure as "a tautology with an added directive appeal."
9. "The Law Behind Law," *Columbia Law Review*, XXIX (1929), 113.
10. "The Duty Problem in Negligence Cases," *Columbia Law Review*, XXVIII (1928), 1014.

tion is not law, regardless of the merits of the judicial process of judgment and the linguistic formulation of that judgment— or the individual responsibility of the particular judicial agent. In paraphrase of Holmes, it might be said that the imperative of the law is not in logic; it is in experience. The logic of judicial judgment presents that judgment to experience for verification; if verified, it can be called law. It is no depreciation of the importance of methodology to assert that a judgment logically derived from premises which are factually incorrect *may* itself be factually incorrect. The authority which the judicial decision evidences will derive from the factual references of the premises upon which it is based; imperation will not flow from the logical or judicial process of judgment itself. As to the nature of those premises, it is interesting to note Holmes's references to "felt necessities" in the sentence following that paraphrased above;[11] this will be a subject for later consideration.

Dickinson emphasizes the distinction between "rules" and "discretion," a classification long employed by Pound. In the lectures already cited, Pound assigned three meanings to law, calling attention to the confusion which results from trying to define all three in terms of any one. These three meanings of law are: (1) the legal order, (2) the body of authoritative guides, and (3) the judicial process.[12] If this distinction is what it appears to be, it does not formulate the factual issue of the legal imperative; for what it asserts factually is that, while the judicial discretion which makes law is *not* authoritative, somehow the law which results from the operation of the judicial process *is* authoritative. This is a hopeful prediction, not a factual assertion.

Perhaps we are rather to be asked to believe that the law accumulates authority because the judgment which proclaims it is grounded in equity, morals, or reason. We do indeed hope

---

11. *The Common Law,* Lecture I.
12. *Op. cit.,* p. 40. Different classifications will be found in others of Pound's works; the problem formulated is the same.

that judicial process is grounded in rational value discrimination, but to assume that rational judgments or moral assertions invoke their own power of imperation is political folly which risks legal suicide. Even to the point of tedium, it must again be insisted that such descriptions leave law subject to authorities which support their claims on factual grounds, even though the fact be but brute force. If one can stomach the definition of the rise of National Socialism in Germany as a "legal revolution," as proclaimed, then the problem posed here will seem artificial.

If any specific meaning is to be conveyed by the term "law," it must therefore be distinguished from those forms of statement which are properly designated entreaty, plea, argument, exhortation, wish, desire, hope. A law does not wish hopefully, it does not entreat, it does not argue; a law commands in form and in fact. That statute which commands in form but not in fact therefore cannot be properly designated a law. To assume to be law that which clearly is not law is as initially misleading and ultimately disillusioning as to believe that the formal pattern of the architect's blueprint is in fact a residence, or that the frosted cardboard box in the baker's window is in fact a wedding cake.

That the law cannot derive its essential imperative quality from either divine or moral sources has been clear in the practice of American and English jurisprudence for a hundred years or more, if not always clear in the minds of the practitioners. The gradual waning of faith in revelation and morals —and even in reason, either singly or in combination, has left legal theory and practice with the embarrassing task of commanding in form, while admitting ignorance or denial of the fact which alone could give ground to the command. "In dethroning our absolutes, we must take care not to exile our imperatives, for after all, we live by them."[13] It must be admitted

13. Alain Locke, "Values and Imperatives," in *American Philosophy Today and Tomorrow* (New York, 1935), p. 313. Locke is one of very few contemporary philosophers who see this problem clearly. "The gravest problem of contemporary philosophy is how to ground some normative principle or criterion

that recent philosophy has indeed exiled prevailing imperatives in the process of dethroning prevailing absolutes. One
result has been that legal speculation more and more turned
inward upon itself, expending its effort on the examination
and manipulation of its own formal symbols and procedures.
Concern for the nature of law in fact, and for the substantial
ground from which law must derive its imperative or enforceability, has become so slight that one could in general anticipate only a reaction of annoyance if such questions were introduced into the introverted studies of schools of legal training.
That the law should manifest a reason for being what it is,
that it should evidence observable and verifiable factual
grounds for the command it attempts to exercise—these are
notions almost alien to those concerned with law, and notions
about which the potential practitioner of law had better not
trouble himself.

The erosion of old absolutes without the discovery or construction of firmer foundations is likely to leave a very shaky
and unsubstantial superstructure. It is not remarkable, nor is
it simply the result of a sudden excess of cynicism, that men
now so generally accept without argument the assumption that
law is no more than a formal pattern for the arrangement of
undisguised power configurations. Legal counselors, both in
practice and in adjudication, seem content with their role as
formal technicians, undisturbed by any necessity to examine
the factual reference of the symbols they so adroitly manipulate. Thus formalized, the law soon comes to lack any discrimination as to the factual grounds which are contributing the
essential imperative to the law. Those who counsel at law

---

of objective validity for values without resort to dogmatism and absolutism on
the intellectual plane, and without falling into their corollaries, on the plane
of social behavior and action, of intolerance and mass coercion" (pp. 315-316).
Locke notes, but without defeatist dismay, the neglect of this problem: "Normally, one would expect a philosophical tradition dominated, as contemporary
American thought has been, by an activist theory of knowledge, to have made
a problem like this central. . . . American thought has moved tangent to the
whole central issue of the normative aspects and problems of value" (pp. 316-
317).

evidence little or no concern as to whether the demands made upon law derive from observable fact, artificial pressure, or the sheer force of individual will to power. While this manipulation of interests and power which passes for legal procedure may, from a perspective of practical expediency, be understandable and even necessary, it is nonetheless deplorable as a substitute for law rationally determined. It is, in fact, another form of legal suicide. The introduction of such quaint concepts as justice and equity into a discussion of legal conflict is likely to bring a glint of cynicism rather than a gleam of interest to the jaundiced eye of today's legal practitioner, unless he assumes that such symbols are being used in rhetorical dissimulation.

The possible consequences of such artificiality in legal procedure are not immediately evident (in fact, they are probably circumvented) when the procedure is confined to a social structure in which rules of order have already achieved a high degree of autonomy through homogeneity of institutional organization. But when the procedure is extended to encompass facts not so institutionally ordered, as in international adjudication, the frailty of artificiality becomes glaringly apparent—and dangerous.

In the presence of this artificiality, power has assumed the status of significant symbol. It is as if the very use of the symbol itself opened vistas once invisible, as if old problems restated with new symbols became immediately clear. Law is the form; power is the force. Law is then but a formalization of manipulations and configurations of power interests, and monopolies of power will contribute to the law whatever power of imperation it manifests. This current form of the problem of the authority of law is even more discouraging than the older statements which tried to describe that authority in terms of divine revelation or reason or moral principles, for now we are apparently trying to make ourselves believe that there is really no problem of the source and ground of that authority.

The problem, however, remains; the history of events will

not allow us for long to ignore the fact that law, as constitutive of those principles of action which men obey in social intercourse, is determined finally by the evidence of an imperative whose source is matched in obscurity only by its effectiveness when called into action. It does not seem naïve to ask: "Why are laws obeyed?" This is in effect to ask what makes a law a law. More pertinent to legal speculation would be the question: "On what grounds can it be anticipated that this law will be obeyed?"; for it is clear that if some reasonable assurance of obedience cannot be assumed, the law will in effect not be a law at all, and the process of enforcement and adjudication will be an embarrassment of futility. There appears little need to point out that this problem is indeed crucial to any social order of any magnitude whatever.

It is saying very little to remark that the nature of fact is neither determined nor altered by a selection or change of symbolic designation. An imperative under any other name is an imperative still; if the nature of the fact which has been called the imperative of law is obfuscated and unclear, it will not be rendered more understandable by calling it another name. There have been many attempts to clarify the factual situation which controls the effectiveness of law; some of these have been more fruitful than the frequent attempts to substitute impassioned conscience for analysis of fact. Many of the significant contributions to our understanding of the factual nature of law have thus come from some of the explorations of the concepts of social contract and sovereignty, the contribution nonetheless important in some instances because negative in character. By far the greater majority of writers, however, seem content to adopt the current symbol being used to designate the unexplored fact, apparently hoping thereby to escape the troublesome problem of clarifying the difficult factual premise of their construction.

Taste in symbols has evidenced all the whimsy of fashion. For Blackstone, the imperative of English law followed from the fortuitous circumstance that legal construction was a discovery and writing out of the laws of nature which conformed to the will of God.

> This law of nature, being coeval with mankind, and dictated by God himself, is of course superior in obligation to any other. It is binding over all the globe, in all countries, and at all times; no human laws are of any validity, if contrary to this; and such of them as are valid derive all their force, and all their authority, mediately or immediately, from this original.[14]

If it should be thought that Blackstone's reliance upon a beneficent deity represents a simplicity of conception confined to his age, it might be well to consider the implications of the report of a conference of the Federal Council of Churches held in 1947 in which the important legal concept of property was given this basic premise: "Property represents a trusteeship under God."[15]

Yet, for all the disparagement to which such statements are now customarily subjected, they are hardly less descriptive than the concept which has of recent times borne the weight of symbolizing the legal imperative: sovereignty. While Bentham and Austin did great service in emphasizing the essential nature of law as command, neither was apparently much interested in exploring the factual basis of that command. Theories of sovereignty based on social contract were not tenable, and in the absence of further exploration legal theory contented itself with the hearty affirmation that law derived its imperative from the will of the sovereign, or the agent thereof, and proceeded to the elaboration of the legal superstructure with introspective zeal. The concept of sovereignty assumed a geographical and nationalistic denotation, and the question of the imperative of law went by default. After all, everybody knew what sovereignty was; it was the will of the state, or the will of the people, or something like that. Prob-

---

14. *Commentaries* (London, 1809), I, 27.
15. For a contemporary statement of the Scholastic view, see Francis Peter LeBuffe and James Vincent de Paul Hayes, *The American Philosophy of Law* (4th ed.; New York, 1947). This work modestly claims to be *the* American philosophy of law, all others being castigated as "alien."

ably the most succinct statement of this point of view is that of Jellinek: "The rights and duties of individuals receive their potency and authority from grounds set forth in objective law. The State finds the grounds for its own rights and duties in itself."[16]

Throughout the period of the development of national states, this casual assumption of national sovereignty as the source of the legal imperative allowed systems of law to attain intricate internal development by the simple expedient of establishing legal systems as equally nationalistic. Thus, the entire problem of the ground or source of law was designated as political and could be ignored by those concerned with legalistic interpretation. This alone accounts for the amazing fact that, despite the rapid and extensive development of government, it is possible to read an almost endless number of works on law and jurisprudence which never so much as mention the legal functions of legislation and administration or, if they take cognizance of the existence of these legal pro-

16. *Gesetz und Verordnung* (Freiburg, 1887), p. 196. Compare Bentham's cavalier assertion that the fact of the establishment of government he assumes as "notorious, and the necessity of it as alike obvious and incontestable" (*An Introduction to the Principles and Morals of Legislation*, p. 214 n. 1).

The fiction of the "personality" of the state, so effectively elaborated by Jellinek, was an important revision of the corporate theory of state and law; it represented a significant advance from the dubious metaphysical presuppositions of Hegel. The "cultural context" emphasis of sociology of law is the only significant development in legal philosophy in the recent past. The reference to institutional structures as the ground of the authority of law had the distinct advantage of factual rather than fictitious reference. Georges Gurvitch has perhaps expressed this most clearly: "The imperative of law . . . is characterized by two different marks: its character as established by a qualified authority which is not identical with the authority of the rule itself, and second, the actual effectiveness of the rule in a given social milieu. . . . It is easy to see that the 'authorities' usually cited as source of positive law—rules, custom, judicial practice, convention, statute, etc.—do not in themselves give any guarantee to the individual of the actual effectiveness of the rule in question" (*L'Idée du Droit Social* [Paris, 1932], p. 133). (Gurvitch distinguishes carefully sociology of law from sociological jurisprudence and sociological *theory* of law. See "Major Problems of the Sociology of Law," *Journal of Social Philosophy*, VI [1941], 197-215.)

Ehrlich even went so far as to deny individual law, asserting that all law was descriptive of associations. It is precisely here, it seems to me, that sociological-context jurisprudence betrays its own descriptive inadequacy, but at the same time it contributes a significant revision of the problem of the authority of law (*Fundamental Principles of the Sociology of Law*, trans. Walter L. Moll [Cambridge, Mass., 1936]). See below, chap. vii.

cedures, give them but the most cavalier attention. The most common expression of this lack of concern usually describes legislation as the source of "written law."[17] It is becoming increasingly evident what the acceptance of this vague and ill-conceived idea of sovereignty as a sufficient ground of the imperative of law has meant to legal theory. It was a happy holiday from worry as long as the legalist could with nationalist fervor assert that his "sovereign"—whatever it was—was rational and beneficent and therefore a good and adequate source of the necessary authority of law. "The happiness of the people, therefore, is the only true end of government. No ruler does avow, no ruler dares avow, any other."[18] There is not, however, enough fervor in the most optimistic of jurists to obscure the unavoidable and deplorable fact that sovereigns do indeed command for purposes other than the happiness and welfare of the people. Sovereigns in the form of political leaders may be vicious, irrational, and ruthless. Sovereignty, in the form of the will of a people—whatever that may mean—may be stupid, irrational, ruthless, or horribly mistaken. What then of the law which derives its authority from this sovereign source?

Precisely this kind of predicament has been described by Ernst Fraenkel in an exposition of the status of law under National Socialism in Germany; it is an alarming historical illustration of the poverty of undefined sovereignty as support of legal authority.

> The entire legal system has become an instrument of the political authorities. . . . It must be presumed that all spheres of life are to be subjected to regulation by law.

17. E.g., Holland, *The Elements of Jurisprudence* (5th ed.; Oxford, 1890), pp. 55-56: "In legislation, both the contents of the rule are devised, and legal force is given to it, by simultaneous acts of the sovereign power which produces 'written law.' All the other law sources produce what is called 'unwritten law,' to which the sovereign authority gives its whole legal force, but not its contents, which are derived from popular tendency, professional discussion, judicial ingenuity, or otherwise, as the case may be. Rules thus developed obtain the force of law by complying with the standards which the State exacts from such rules before it gives them binding force."
As for the lack of attention to administrative law, see below, pp. 116-119.
18. Sir William Markby, *The Elements of Law* (6th ed.; Oxford, 1905), p. 30.

Whether the decision in an individual case is made in accordance with the law or with 'expediency' is entirely in the hands of those in whom the sovereign power is vested. Their sovereignty consists in the very fact that they determine the permanent emergency.[19]

In this statement Fraenkel equates sovereignty and power; since the power to which he refers was sheer and ruthless force, the implication is clear. There was nothing in the prevailing concept of sovereignty itself to distinguish legal authority from monopoly of force, and a legal system which purports to derive its authority from such a notion of sovereignty will be at the complete mercy of any configuration of power strong enough or ruthless enough to establish itself in control. There is a suggestion elsewhere in Fraenkel's analysis that the destruction of legal authority in Germany resulted from an absence of order in the institutional structures of that society; this is a point for later and more detailed consideration.

Fraenkel also illustrates the futility of "ideological" support of the false foundation of sovereignty. The potentially strongest group in Germany, the Social Democrats, was rendered ineffective by its adherence to an unrealistic concept of authority.

The tragedy of the Marxian political movement in Germany lies in part in the fact that they became, in spite of many warnings of their founders, the victims of their belief in Natural Law even under the rule of capitalism. . . . Social Democracy, which originally had torn the ideological veil from the economic system of capitalistic society, in turn witnessed its ideology being unveiled as utopian by National Socialism. The premature attempt to realize an order based on utopian Natural Law was fatal to Social Democracy.[20]

By contrast, consider the nature of a truly dual state in which the ideological rhetoric is retained but in no wise allowed to interfere with the establishment of sovereign power in the form of sheer force.

19. *The Dual State* (New York, 1941), p. 57.
20. *Ibid.*, pp. 131-132.

>There is not the slightest thought of erecting a system of
law which would bind the leadership of the Party, which
would formally or practically limit their power to take
any steps which they might deem necessary. . . . The reform movement does not fundamentally change the
totalitarian quality of the Soviet system of law. It miti-
gates the harshness of the system, and thereby increases
the popular acceptance of it. . . . The Soviet leadership remains the master, and not the servant, of the legal order.[21]

Before we smirk too smugly at the efforts of Austin, Holland, and others of their period, we might be well advised to
consider whether in the plethora of our contemporary jargon
we can discern any more acceptable definition of legal authority than they adduced. The arguments which grounded the
imperative in sovereignty, while ill-conceived as descriptive
explanations, at least had the merit of appealing to reason. It is
difficult to hold a brief for some of the theories which try to
objectify moral prejudice in terms of natural law; but in many
instances reference to natural law represented a sincere effort
to establish principles of legal order in rational value discriminations. It is both incorrect and unjust to lump together the
attempts to pervert the concept of natural law to the uses of a
sacerdotal bid for power with the quite different effort to
equate natural law and reason. The assumptions that reason
prevails in the affairs of men and that men may be expected to
behave like rational beings if given liberty to do so may be unrealistic political premises, but they are also sublime ones and
surely preferable to the unpromising view that there is no
alternative to the establishment of authority by sheer, undisciplined force. Good or even sublime motives, however, are
not a sufficient safeguard for law against the depredations of
monopolies of power; nor is it enough to show that the principles of law are derived from reasonable or acceptable value
discriminations. The imperative of law cannot be established
on moral grounds, and the realization of this fact but increases

21. Harold J. Berman, "Law Reform in the Soviet Union," *The American Slavic and East European Review,* XV (1956), 189.

our sympathy for those who think they are so doing, when they are ultimately faced with the arbitrariness and expediency of unlegislated force.

If the circumstances appear bleak in respect to the status of national systems of law, they are even more distressing in that area which has come to dominate our attention: international law. Austin was much more perceptive on this point than most of his overzealous critics; he recognized more clearly than they the results to law of his acceptance of a nationalistic concept of sovereignty. Austin refused to give international law the status of positive law; in the terms we have used here, this was tantamount to denying it the status of law at all. He interpreted international law as merely a series of agreements entered into by equally authoritative sovereign powers, enforced and maintained only at the sufferance and will of the participating sovereignties. International law does not, on this view, represent a contract in any legal sense, inasmuch as there is no describable agency of enforcement. International law evidences no imperative, and its propositions are not commands; it is, therefore, not law in any factual sense.[22]

22. See Holland, *op. cit.*, pp. 114-115: "But there is a third kind of law which it is for many reasons convenient to coordinate with the former two kinds, although it can indeed be described as law only by courtesy, since the rights with which it is concerned cannot properly be described as legal. It is that body of rules, usually described as International law, which regulates the rights which prevail between State and State (*civitas* and *civitas*).

"The difference between these three kinds of law, Private, Public and International, depends upon the presence or absence of an arbiter of the rights of the parties. . . . It is plain that if Law be defined as we have defined it, a political arbiter by which it can be enforced is of its essence, and law without an arbiter is a contradiction in terms. Convenient therefore as is on many accounts the phrase 'International law' to express those rules of conduct in accordance with which, either in consequence of their express consent or in pursuance of the usage of the civilized world, nations are expected to act, it is impossible to regard these rules as being in reality anything more than the moral code of nations."

See also Herman Finer, *America's Destiny* (New York, 1947), pp. 76-78: "International law is not the product of legislatures like those which make statutes in the various nations, because an international legislature does not exist. . . . The defect is that the right to make war is at the pure discretion or caprice of any nation. . . . In this system there is no common superior, in the form of an arbiter or judge or court continuously in session with a jurisdiction at once compulsory, authoritative, and enforceable."

Cf. J. L. Brierly, *The Outlook for International Law* (Oxford, 1945), p. 21: "A system professing to be one of Law, which yet is incapable of making the

Perhaps the most deplorable result of our acceptance of a vague concept of national sovereignty as the only source of legal authority has been that our reasoning in respect to the principles of international law has progressed very little since those principles were formulated in 1625 by Grotius. There manifestly has never been a sovereignty which could be assumed as the source of the authority of international law. Thus, those who continue to insist that there is, or should be, such a thing as international law are forced to adduce some other source for its authority. The only rationalization available seems to be that of falling back on the always dubious and now surely outworn concept of "natural law," the very ground assumed by Grotius.[23] Maine long ago described clearly how the acceptance of the Grotian theory is dependent upon a concept of territorial sovereignty.

> The theory of International Law assumes that commonwealths are, relatively to each other, in a state of nature; but the component atoms of a natural society must, by the fundamental assumption, be insulated and independent of each other.[24]

There is no point in belaboring the fact that mere reference to nationalistic sovereignty is not a sufficient ground for the necessary imperative of law. Even within the limits of a nation itself, the fact of sovereignty cannot merely be assumed; if the reference is to any kind of fact, that fact must be defined and described, else the authority of law will remain without factual reference, an unenviable position in situations of power manipulation. Without such factual reference, law can hardly claim to be a principle of order, the guarantor of justice and security, or representative of the rule of reason in social organi-

---

most elementary use of physical force, is entitled to very little respect and hardly deserves to be described as legal at all."

23. Cf. Pollock, *Essays in the Law* (London, 1922), p. 63: "We must either admit that modern International law is a law founded on cosmopolitan principles of reason, a true living offshoot of the Law of Nature, or ignore our own most authoritative exposition of it."

For a recent statement of the natural law doctrine, see LeBuffe and Hayes, *op. cit.*

24. *Ancient Law* (9th ed.; London, 1883), p. 172.

zation. On the contrary, it cannot lay claim to being more than a useful tool, and to admit such status is to add perfidy to indigence.[25]

In international affairs, the inadequacy is more obvious and more critical. After World War II, in the trial of war criminals at Nuremberg, we witnessed an unprecedented effort on the part of the prosecution to demonstrate that there were good and sufficient grounds for indictment and conviction, and that the executions were thus the administration of a legal imperative and not the summary act of a military victor.[26] Our moral

25. See, e.g., Pollock, *A First Book in Jurisprudence* (London, 1918), pp. 28-29: "For most practical purposes the citizens of a State, and to a considerable extent, though not altogether, lawyers and magistrates also, have not to concern themselves with thinking what those foundations [political and social foundations of law] are. Their business is to learn and know, so far as needful for their affairs, what rules the State does undertake to enforce and administer, whatever the real or professed reasons for those rules may be. . . . Law is enforced by the State because it is law; it is not law merely because the State enforces it. But the further pursuit of this subject seems to belong to the philosophy of Politics rather than of Law. . . . If it be asked what is a commonwealth in general, that is a question of political and not of legal science. If it be asked whether the definition covers the law of nations, the answer is that it more or less approximately does so just so far as the relations of sovereign States to one another can be regarded as analogous to those of citizens in a State. A definition has no business to pre-judge the question how far that is the case."

It is small wonder that our prevailing concepts of sovereignty and authority are so muddled. Insofar as any sense can be made of Pollock's remarks, importance lies in the demand for the treatment of relations between states as analogous to the relations of individuals within a state. Since such an analogy is a manifest absurdity, it cannot provide legal theory with an excuse to turn off the problem as political or philosophical. "When we say that the British Commonwealth of Nations or even Great Britain alone has moral obligations toward the United States or France, we are making use of a fiction. By virtue of this fiction international law deals with nations as though they were individual persons, but nothing in the sphere of moral obligations corresponds to this legal concept. . . . In any case, the reference to a moral rule of conduct requires an individual conscience from which it emanates, and there is no individual conscience from which what we call the international morality of Great Britain or any other nation could emanate" (Hans Morgenthau, *Politics Among Nations* [New York, 1948], p. 188).

26. Thus, Robert H. Jackson, chief of counsel for the United States at the Nuremberg trials, there argued: "Unless we are prepared to abandon every principle of growth for International Law, we cannot deny that our own day has the right to institute customs and to conclude agreements that will themselves become sources of a newer and strengthened International Law. You judge, therefore, under an organic act which represents the wisdom, the sense of justice, and the will of nineteen governments, representing an overwhelming majority of all civilized people" (*Trial of War Criminals* [Department of State Publication 2420, Washington, 1945], p. 9).

The desperation of this effort to find an imperative, a legal authority for the contemplated prosecution, is evident in the re-assertion of the fiction described

sentiments, profoundly abhorrent of the acts of the German state, our sense of decent behavior in relations with other men, our fear of this national and wholesale aberration—these are not here in question, however commendable, and however strongly we continue to hold these moral beliefs and preferences. What is in question is whether there is any factual basis for the claim of legal authority. It is easy enough to recognize that, in the absence of such factual ground, law becomes the prey of political power; it is less palatable to recognize that a temporary surge of moral resentment is no better substitute as a basis for legal authority than is any other monopoly of power. Execution by command of power, be it political, moral, or otherwise, is not legal but summary execution. Perhaps the experience of these trials has forced upon our attention a reconsideration of the ground and source of the imperative which can provide legal authority for the execution of the law. Unless we can clearly discriminate such a source of imperative authority, law must admit that it derives whatever force it has from a prevailing monopoly of power wielding a monopoly of force. It should be noted that the inadequacy of the heretofore prevailing concept of sovereignty as the source of this authority was demonstrated in these trials, since the doctrine served neither as an argument for the prosecution nor a defense for the accused.[27]

---

by Maine and Morgenthau. The fiction was asserted as the ground of the purported legal authority in the face of overt and persistent manifestations of fact which belied the fiction. No contortion of terminology can obscure the inadequacy of such a claim to legal authority; "organic act" conveys no meaning when there was in fact nothing organic about the agreement; it is a rather weird departure from historical juristic concepts to speak of customs as being "instituted" deliberately.

See the remark on fictions, p. 121, nn. 24, 25.

27. See Sheldon Glueck, *The Nuremberg Trial and Aggressive War* (New York, 1946), p. 53 n.: "Those statesmen and lawyers who have raised the concept of 'Sovereignty' to the status of some holy fetish have ignored historical facts. The more rigid, legalistic notions of sovereignty are of comparatively late (nineteenth-century) origin or re-birth. . . . Practical considerations in our era, such as the fact that sovereigns of certain nations have several times clearly demonstrated their self-appointed divine right to trample over the territory and lives of neighboring peoples in violation of solemn treaty obligations, and particularly the sobering fact of the advent of the atomic bomb, should bring about a reformation of the theory of national sovereignty."

The realization that what had purported to be factual ground for the authority of law was, at least as defined, not factual at all, should have suggested a re-examination of the facts relevant to political and legal authority. However, an age supposedly obsessed with factual analysis turned doggedly to yet another contrary-to-fact hypothesis in the effort to derive legal authority from moral preference.

CHAPTER III

AUTHORITY AS
MORAL FICTION

*Law must inevitably be greatly superior to Positive
Morality in definiteness and consistency; since in the case
of moral rules there is no judicial process by which doubts
as to what the accepted rule is on any question can be
authoritatively settled, and no legislative process by
which any divergence from what, in the opinion of
thoughtful persons,* ought *to be established morality, can
be at once and decisively removed* .... *the moral code of
a modern country has come to be necessarily inferior as
an intelligible system to its law, because in the case of the
former every man is encouraged to think himself a judge,
there is no final court of appeal, and no one can admit
any external legislation.*[1]

L AW continues to speak with authority and in authoritative
tones. Despite law's criticism of itself, despite its disdainful rejection of the claims of divine revelation, sovereign dele-
gation, moral jurisdiction, and even sometimes the rule of
reason, yet law still claims authority. The imperative so vigorously rejected at one level shows up at another; the assumption
which arouses heated censure is casually accepted when expressed with another symbol. We noted that Dickinson, for example, would have none of the notion that there is a "higher
law" behind the law of a particular adjudication; yet he feels
compelled to urge that the adjudication must be accepted as
"authoritative." Pound refers to the "authoritative ideal,"
"effective legal action," and what he does knowingly, others do

1. Henry Sidgwick, *The Elements of Politics* (London, 1891), pp. 195, 196.

unwittingly. Jerome Frank, in a book which had a considerable popular appeal, attacked the concept of authority in law with more vigor than discretion.[2] His presentation is somewhat extreme, but the view of legal authority he expounds represents a kind of analysis which has apparently been of some influence, although few who assume this position have such a background of legal training and practice as does Frank. His denunciation of all those who recognize that law must convey an imperative is meant to be scathing, but issues are seldom clarified by the indiscriminate use of bizarre and blatant symbols. Mr. Frank discovers that all who have looked upon the law as authoritative, from Aristotle through and including the Puritans, were very probably suffering from father-worship, victims of a "harsh, authoritative relationship between the father and his children." Suffering from such a complex, these benighted individuals throughout the history of legal speculation have evidenced "a longing to reproduce the father-child pattern, to escape uncertainty and confusion through the rediscovery of a father." Behold the law!

The fact that we have political societies ordered under law —not perfectly, to be sure—attests the labors of those men who recognized that law must be imperative and that, if law is to be other than sheer force, it must justify that imperative on some grounds understandable and acceptable to men. The initial purpose of such an analysis as that of Frank may be worthy, but the result to the analysis of law is vicious.[3] If we are to

2. *Law and the Modern Mind* (New York, 1930).

3. Such burlesques of rational analysis are not directly pertinent to the problem being discussed here, but this kind of thing has become so popular at a certain level that it promises to obfuscate an already difficult subject. In passing, therefore, it is perhaps appropriate to cite an evaluation of this kind of "analysis" by an authority who has given ample evidence that he knows whereof he speaks: "The Oedipus complex lurks like a ghost in the attic, and stamps natural parent-child affection with the sickly tint of 'sexual perversion.' . . . Yet actually the only kind of parent who ever produced sexual fixations in children is of course a sexually obsessed or vulgar and unimaginative parent, in which case the child is fortunate if he escapes with nothing worse than an 'Oedipus complex.' . . . Parental sexual fixations of remembered childhood can be suggested readily enough to neurotic minds, and can be teased up delightfully into the dimensions of a general alibi, but so can anything else. If I can win the confidence of an uncritical person (establish a transference), I

understand the problem of authority in law, it will be through the employment of the usual processes of reason: by careful scrutiny of observable fact, clear analysis, and rigorous distinction of symbols from referents, values from facts, ideals from ideas. Many efforts are necessary to achieve minimum results in such an undertaking; it seems both foolhardy and presumptuous to assume that the men who have employed themselves in this task have been ignorant or obsessed. The facts would seem to bear witness that there are many who have been neither the one nor the other. It would bespeak discretion if we look with overindulgent rather than overcritical eye upon those who have labored at the description of law and its function in society. It is not, however, our purpose here to indulge in historical evaluation, but rather to try to understand what characteristic of law it is that could reasonably satisfy the demand for authority.

The general argument which attempted to establish the imperative of law as deriving from universal or eternal divine law necessitated the acceptance of revelation as the only method of defining that divine law. The method of revelation has been extensively and adequately criticized in legal theory and elsewhere, and it would be tedious to reiterate those argu-

---

can make him believe that he has the soul of a blue heron and can plausibly interpret every dream in such a way as to prove it. I can even 'cure' him by convincing him that he has made a great mistake in trying to be something different from a blue heron, and now he will be happy imitating the habits of that noble bird. He will be whole, having found the light and the true way. . . . The psychoanalytic slang of Oedipus and castration complexes and of overshadowing parental sexual fixations, has filtered into the common consciousness not through the psychological fraternity. . . . Much of this slang has come in by way of cheap journalism, and through books on psychological subjects written by grossly incompetent people whose claim to psychological maturity may rest only upon the fact that they themselves have been made 'whole' by being psychoanalyzed. If the process of being treated for neurosis gives a person mature psychological insight, then to have one's leg broken and set should constitute adequate training for a certificate in surgery. These people have been *converted* to something, and that in itself is almost proof positive of profound psychological distortion and mental bad health. The mind that is suddenly converted to something is a mind without balance, stability, or dependability. It is an unmellow mind. There is ground for extreme skepticism of any adult who suddenly 'gets a new religion' " (W. H. Sheldon, *Psychology and the Promethean Will* [New York, 1963], pp. 162-166).

ments here. Revelation is not a method acceptable to reason; it cannot therefore be acceptable to law. We need not enter into discussion here with those who claim revelation as a proper method; it is sufficient to remark that the method of law is by definition a rational method and can establish its grounds only upon facts rationally verifiable.

The claim of sovereignty has already been discussed in the preceding chapter. It has been clear for some time that sovereignty (if it means no more than it has thus far been made to mean) will not suffice as a ground for the necessary imperative of law; that it has seemed to suffice for nationalistic systems of law has been due to the fact that the symbol was not questioned, and the concept of legal authority was lost in the clamor of noisily developing sovereignties.[4] There have been numerous attempts to give the concept of sovereignty rational description, both before and after the enunciation of the "command theory" by Austin.[5] These efforts have not, on the whole, been characterized by marked success; but they at least made an extremely important contribution to the investigation of the imperative of law in the various efforts to explore and define the fact of "will." Sovereignty, as the source of authority in the state, apparently had to be defined as will; therefore, the authority of the state which transmits itself through law is an expression of the will of the state. This traditional statement, of course, is not illuminating unless the terms "will" and "state" have some definiteness of meaning, and it is at this point that most descriptions of this nature bog down. Even the effort to delimit state to a denotation geographically or territorially determined has not been successful

4. "It has been seriously proposed to delete the word 'sovereignty' from our lexicons. But the question of what should be substituted always arises. . . . What shall we call the substitute for the thing we have thrown out? What is it that takes the place of sovereignty in a world of nonsovereign states? After all, is it the word we wish to throw out, or the concept, or the implications of the concept or the word?" (C. E. Merriam, *op. cit.*, p. 38).

I shall retain the word "sovereignty" and try to make some factual sense of it (see below, chap. vii).

5. For a very good exposition of the various meanings given to sovereignty, see W. J. Rees, "The Theory of Sovereignty Restated," in *Philosophy, Politics and Society* (New York, 1956), pp. 52-82.

because of contradictory interpretations of "will." The democratic representative declares himself to be the representative of the will of the people, the only rightful source of sovereignty. The dictator asserts that, as leader, he is the embodiment or spokesman of the will of the historic state; his will is the source of sovereign authority. An oligarchy may lay claim to authority, and hence claim to speak for the state, through possession of the instruments of power.[6]

As noted above, by far the most persistent and influential of the claimants to the authority necessary to provide a legal imperative have been natural law and natural rights. The history of these concepts and their influence on legal thought presents a complicated and fascinating subject for discussion, but attention here will be confined to the implications for the general problem of the imperative. The most significant of these is the fact that the reference to natural law as a ground for the authority of civil law represents a direct appeal to morals. Whether natural law has been described in terms of a rule of justice, the rule of reason, *lex aeterna,* utility, or the unalienable birthright of individuals, each concept represents an effort to establish an objective ground or source for the authority of law, and the objectivity of the ground supposedly derives from its moral or "reasonable" connotation.

Natural law is the phoenix of legal speculation; however often it is criticized to extinction, it rises again, an old spirit in a new and vigorous body. Untouched by the scathing fires of ridicule, the law of nature appears anew as a "higher law prevailing in every legal state," the hope of international law and order.[7] More than forty years ago, Morris Cohen asserted that

6. See chap. ii n. 21.
7. See, for example, "Statement of Essential Human Rights," *The Annals of the American Academy of Political and Social Science,* XXIV (1946); and, of course, the many sources which use natural law doctrine as a support for the imposition of religious or personal dogma.
See also Frank D. Graham, *Social Goals and Economic Institutions* (Princeton, 1942), pp. 255-256: "The reliance on natural law, with its implications for sociological method, has had a most unfortunate influence on the development of all the social sciences, particularly economics. However vigorously the assertion may, in some quarters, be denied, it is fair to say that the doctrine still

"to defend a doctrine of natural rights today requires either insensibility of the world's progress or else considerable courage in the face of it";[8] perhaps there are still men of courage. Events sometimes rouse men to a courage thought cannot evoke; thus, affirmations that the ground of law and order in society rests upon the preservation of human rights have recently been made by those who not long ago were vehemently annihilating as unrealistic the whole doctrine of natural law and natural rights. What this seems to indicate is simply that in the face of a crucial threat to the system of legal order, there is available no more cogent argument than the most appealing and respectable of the traditional descriptions of law, even though that very argument has been repeatedly rejected in periods of more deliberative appraisal. It is doubly damaging that law should be supported on grounds which we have every reason to believe will be rejected by reason when practice demands verification. There is no reason for believing that efforts to derive an imperative for international law from "natural law" or "natural rights" will be any more successful today than other such efforts since the days of Grotius. The conflict between appeals to natural rights and prevailing concepts of sovereignty marks the final absurdity characteristic of almost every recent instance of international dispute.

A rational man cannot believe what his reason has indicated to be false or, at the very least, unreliable. It appears safe to

---

survives as the libido of much of the contemporary work in that field. This is the principal source of its negative character. The shadow of the concept of natural law has almost inevitably caused economic analysis to serve as the unwitting tool of a rationalization of things as they are. The science has thus become not only dismal but slavishly discreet. The nineteenth century conception of the task of the scientist as the discernment of the 'immutable laws' of nature has given support to a methodology of 'pure' description rather than to a study of techniques for the attainment of consciously adopted social ends."

The semantic manipulation of "idealist—materialist" does not alter the fundamental character of the Marxist appeal to natural law. Engels in *Socialism Utopian and Scientific* proclaimed that "nature is the proof of dialectics," and referred to the "peculiar inherent laws" of production as "inexorable natural laws." However distasteful it may be to some proponents of natural-law theory to find themselves thus associated with Marxist doctrine, the dogmas are nevertheless suspiciously similar.

8. *Philosophical Review*, XXV (1916), 761.

assert that the doctrine of natural law is no longer presented in terms of reference to the "rule of reason." In procedure, the application of the classic norm will inevitably result in determination according to the pragmatic criterion of "under the circumstances" rather than in consideration of the more speculative ideal of "reasonable man." The appeal to natural law has become clearly and unmistakably an appeal to a moral basis for the imperative of law, and this development has at least served the purpose of clarifying the confusion between law and morals which has plagued legal speculation and ethical theory throughout the course of Western history. It was an absence of distinction inherited from the Greeks[9] and vastly confused by Christian tradition; the assumed correlation of reason, morals, and law became so fixed in our thinking, our terminology, and our analysis that it persists to this day to obscure the facts of law in mixed terminology which symbolizes confused concepts.[10] This problem is very perplexing, compli-

9. It is uncritical hindsight which reads into the words of the ancients distinctions and discriminations which in fact did not occur to them. The discrimination of such concepts as civil law, divine law, moral law, and natural law is the product of progressive analysis. In one sense, the stage of development of a given society might well be evaluated on the basis of the degree of such discrimination which it evidences. A great deal of interpretative error of this kind has characterized references to Greek philosophy. For clarification of Greek legal concepts, see *The Administration of Justice from Homer to Aristotle*, by R. J. Bonner and G. Smith (Chicago, 1930), esp. Vol. I.

10. There is a kind of irreducible ambiguity in legal speculation like Kelsen's, which on the one hand declares independence of morals and proclaims a kind of naïve ethical relativism, but which derives its ultimate imperative from an undefined *Grundnorm*. If, as Lauterpacht suggests, this basic norm is simply a methodological device, it can hardly be a source of legal authority. "There is in it no such absolute element which it would necessarily contain if it were grounded in a material ethical value, for instance, in that of justice" (Hans Lauterpacht, "Kelsen's Pure Science of Law," *Modern Theories of Law* [London, 1933], p. 111).

This is a most interesting comment on Kelsen's view. In 1933 Kelsen published an article on "Die platonische Gerechtigkeit" in *Kantstudien*. The following were the two concluding paragraphs in that article, but when Kelsen republished it in a volume of essays, *What is Justice?* (Berkeley, 1957), pp. 82-109, these two paragraphs were conspicuously omitted.

"This philosophy which has led from Platonic love through Platonic truth to Platonic justice, and which operates under the compulsion of an immanent legality, shows us that rational science can never give an answer to the question concerning the nature of justice. Philosophy not only fails to give an answer but leads to the conclusion that the question itself is not valid. The final position it will take in all its different forms is that there is no such thing as absolute justice: it cannot be determined conceptually. Such an ideal is an

cated by usage, tradition, and in many cases by the mystic mantle of righteousness or conscience. However, the distinction between law and morals is, in a very real sense, the determining factor in the description of the legal imperative; if this distinction cannot be made and if it cannot be maintained, then the law will have to be defined as very different from what we now assume it to be.

A consideration of the relation of morals and law is therefore a necessary negative step in the analysis of the authority of law. The description of the relation will not in itself provide a description of legal authority. On the other hand, the nature of a real legal imperative will continue to remain obscure as long as we persist in the illusion that moral assumptions or principles will contribute to the legal order an imperative which our reason clearly tells us the moral cannot contribute—to law or to anything else. In the face of a strong current of criticism of the command theory of law, it may be somewhat hazardous to argue that law by definition must exhibit a real imperative. A real imperative—legal authority—must be defined as a command which, upon demand, could exert the coercion necessary to fulfil the command in action. Only thus

---

illusion. There are only interests and conflicts of interests, which are either compromised into harmony or left in a state of strife. Within the sphere of reason the idea of justice vanishes, leaving only the idea of peace. The concept which can stand the scrutiny of reason is not justice but peace.

"Justice resides, nevertheless, despite all reason, in man's heart. The need and the desire of man for a justice that is more than compromise and more than mere restraining of potential enemies defy the attempts of reason to exorcise the ideal of justice as a dangerous illusion. Man's belief in a higher law and in a supreme good remains forever unshaken. History is a witness to the actual indestructibility of this belief. If the belief be an illusion, then is illusion indeed stronger than reality. For most men—perhaps for all men—there are some problems which cannot be translated into theoretical puzzles to be solved by analysis of concepts, some issues which cannot be posed as questions to be answered by reason. That men will ever be satisfied with the answer of the Sophists is not likely. Men will continue to search out the religious road along which Plato struggled, even though it be a road of blood and tears" (my translation; pp. 399-400 from "Platonic Justice," Ethics, XLVIII [1938], 367-400.

Apparently, this was an effort to assert a "material ethical value," and what a confusing and ambiguous statement it is. If anything like this is to be asserted as the ground of the juridical norm, then the authority of that norm is indeed shaky, unreliable, and indefinable.

can the command be accepted as a real rather than a formal command,[11] and only thus can a law be accepted as a real law rather than simply a pretense or a miscarriage. This definition of law indicates immediately the distinction which it is necessary to maintain between moral principles and legal commands. No moral action can result from circumstances in which the agent is subject to coercion. Morality is properly attributed to an act in which an individual evaluates and elects an alternative of behavior because he judges that alternative to be "reasonable," "best," "right," or "good." Rational systems of morality do not command; they exhort. The moralist must not command his listeners to action, for if he were to attempt to enforce his command by coercion, he would cease immediately to be a moralist in the effort to be a legislator. The expression "moral imperative," therefore, implies a restriction of imperativeness so severe that it deprives the word and the expression of exact meaning. If the influence of duty or reason or good will were, in fact, such as to constitute a "command," the problem of morals and law would be considerably simplified—but, contrary to our ordinary assumption, the problem of the imperative of law would not thereby be solved, perhaps not even clarified.

The law must command; it cannot be mere exhortation. *What* constitutes the ground of the authority of law is the subject of discussion here; but it is hardly to be denied that the law *can* and *does* legitimately command for a number of reasons which could in no wise be acceptable as the basis of moral action; among these might be mentioned expediency and the rule of the majority. It is clear that the law does command for such non-moral reasons; it is not clear why the law has the authority to issue such commands.

The recognition that systems of morals and systems of law

11. It is this necessary factual distinction which indicates that clarification of the so-called "logic of imperatives," to which some attention is now being devoted in certain quarters, is not likely to contribute much to the definition of the legal imperative, although it may well have certain applications to procedural problems.

cannot be superimposed or correlated has appeared now and then in the history of legal and ethical speculation, but it is apparently an idea so repugnant to the wishful mind of man that he rationalizes his observation in the direction of desire. It would indeed simplify matters if the legal and the moral were coterminous; this would be the kingdom of heaven. In fact, such a condition properly describes the kingdom of heaven; it is only in divine law that such a happy conjunction of reason, morals, and law can be postulated. The circumstances in which law is compelled to function are not such as to satisfy the requirements of a kingdom in which divine law realizes such perfection. *Lex aeterna* must become *lex naturalis* if it is to make any sense in mundane affairs—and the problem of an authority for *lex naturalis* is before us once more. The derivation of law from morals can be accomplished only in the postulation of the ideal or in the perfection of the divine.

Hobbes, together with Grotius, is generally credited with the major contribution in distinguishing natural law from divine law, an important step in the analysis of political authority. Hobbes experienced in his analysis the same kind of linguistic and conceptual difficulties that plague us today in the association of law and morals. As a consequence, it is very difficult to evaluate and co-ordinate various aspects of Hobbes's thinking. He saw clearly that in a "state of nature" there could be no such thing as law; hence, natural law he defined as that which was dictated by the reason of man.

> Therefore *true reason* is a certain law; which, since it is no less a part of human nature, than any other faculty or affection of the mind, is also termed natural. Therefore the law of nature, that I may define it, is the dictate of right reason. . . . By right reason in the natural state of men, I understand not, as many do, an infallible faculty, but the act of reasoning, that is, the peculiar and true ratiocination of every man concerning those actions of his, which may either redound to the damage or benefit of his neighbors.[12]

12. *The English Works of Thomas Hobbes*, ed. Molesworth (London, 1839-1845), II, *Philosophical Rudiments Concerning Government and Society*, p. 16.

It might be said that he made the distinction of divine law, civil law, and moral obligation as clear as could be expected of anyone enmeshed in the concepts and terminology of his age.

> They confound *laws* with *right,* who continue still to do what is permitted by *divine right,* notwithstanding it be forbidden by the *civil law.* . . . That which may be done by *divine right,* doth no whit hinder why the same may not be forbidden by the civil laws. . . . *Natural* is that which God hath declared to all men by his *eternal word* born with them, to wit, their *natural reason;* and this is that law, which in this whole book I have endeavored to unfold. . . . Whence it follows, that no civil law whatsoever which tends not to a reproach of the Deity . . . can possibly be against the law of nature. For though the law of nature forbid theft, adultery, etc.; yet if the civil law command us to invade anything, that invasion is not theft, adultery, etc.[13]

He would not tolerate the claims of those who sought to supplement reason with revelation: "But this pretense of covenant with God, is so evident a lie, even in the pretender's own conscience, that it is not only an act of an unjust, but also of a vile and unmanly disposition." [14]

Hobbes's independence of traditional patterns of analysis was probably exhibited most sharply in his recognition that morals could not provide an adequate foundation for law. He belittled "conscience," not only as mere opinion, but as mere "private opinion." He knew that opinion ought to be verifiable and, therefore, that any opinion which could rightfully claim the status of knowledge would in some sense be "public opinion." It was on the basis of this analysis that he declared, "Law is the public Conscience, by which he hath already undertaken to be guided." In short, law is derived from public opinion—that is, public knowledge—which Hobbes assumed to be the essential reason of man.

Numerous points of issue can be raised in respect to

13. *Op. cit.,* pp. 185-191. Compare Kant's appraisal of divine law and civil law, below p. 58.
14. *Op. cit.,* III, *Leviathan,* p. 161.

Hobbes's description of the necessary administrative organization of the state; much of his thinking here was dictated by his position in history. The most suggestive aspects of his work were his analysis of the state as essentially an organization and administration of power, his recognition that there were no rights such as those vested in property except as granted under law, and the implication that the function of social organization under law is to provide peaceful access to useful instruments. "The passions that incline men to peace, are fear of death; desire of such things as are necessary to commodious living; and a hope by their industry to obtain them." [15] The function of law is thus utilitarian, not moral, although Hobbes often falls into the terminological pattern of his day and declares that the laws of nature are the "sum of moral philosophy." Yet he carefully distinguishes the moral obligations to fulfil contracts from the legal command which enforces contracts. Hobbes came closer than subsequent thought would indicate to understanding that the things necessary to "commodious living" are comprehended under the general concept of property, that it is only within an *institutionally* organized social structure that such property-objects can become available to the purposes of man; therefore, the function of law is the ordering of the institutional structure of society in such a way as to provide man with the instruments of living. From this perspective, Hobbes saw that peace was not so much an end of law as law itself. It was for this reason that he was so harsh in respect to violations of the sovereignty which comprised the legal power of the state.[16]

It is the task of the historian to trace the pattern of events and figures in the development of thought; suffice it to say that the age of reason became after Hobbes the age of faith. Men eulogized the uses of reason—and used reason to support dogmatic moral doctrines in philosophy, politics, and law. It was

15. *Ibid.*, p. 116.
16. Compare also the "harshness" of Kant and Bradley, for example, in the matter of retributive punishment, a position which many of their critics have wholly misunderstood and erroneously tried to pass off as an aberration.

not, as they claimed, that they found in Hobbes an unrealistic description of reason, man, and society; it was rather that they could not give up the dream of a divine correlation of reason, morals, and law. The endowed reason of man, his emotions, his feelings, his inclination to morality—in short, the psychological emphasis which began to characterize philosophical analysis—became the data, not of factual analysis, but rather of an artificial construction designed to support a pre-existing set of moral postulates.[17] The result was very bad psychology, and the source of some very bad epistemology. Typical of this direction of thought was the misnamed Common Sense school of philosophy; better it were called the school of moral sentimentalists. The science of psychology may have derived some impetus from this pragmatic origin, but legal theory suffered immeasurably in this lapse of philosophy from rational analysis to justification of faith.[18]

17. See Carl L. Becker, *The Heavenly City of Eighteenth-Century Philosophers* (New Haven, 1932), e.g., pp. 103-104: "It is apparent that, in professing with so disarming an air of candor to be studying history in order to discover the constant and universal principles of human nature, they are deceiving us, these philosopher-historians. But we can easily forgive them for that, since they are, even more effectively, deceiving themselves. They do not know that the 'man in general' they are looking for is just their own image, that the principles they are bound to find are the very ones they start out with. That is the trick they play on the dead. They unconsciously give themselves away for their insistence on the union of morality and politics. Those who would separate morality and politics, according to Rousseau, know nothing of either. . . . It is only too clear: the philosopher-historians possess the idea of the just and the unjust, they have their 'universal principles' and their 'man in general' well in hand before they start out to explore the field of human experience."
The great volume of utopian speculations of the eighteenth and nineteenth centuries, their tremendous influence on the thought of the period, and indeed the history of adventures in ideal-community experiments, attest the widespread and powerful compulsion of this tour de force identification of reason, morals, political order, and law. See Glenn Negley and J. Max Patrick, *The Quest for Utopia* (New York, 1952, 1962).
18. An instance of the persistence of this kind of distortion in analysis can be seen in Ihering's development of his definition of legal rights as interests, interests being defined as "all that can be of service to us." But the insistence on psychological and subjective interpretation forced him to qualify this description by admitting as a necessary element of rights that the agent take an initiative of *willful* protection of those rights. On the basis of the interest theory, Ihering made an important qualification of Hobbes's sovereign authority: Ihering asserted that the state could make laws to which it itself was subject; such laws would be made on the basis of the self-interest of the state in order to promote security. This makes very good sense if interests are under-

[II]

The most astute, as well as the most influential, figure in
the extended effort to discover in morals the ground of authority was Kant. The great rationalist was in some respects the
greatest rationalizer of them all; all aspects of his philosophy
were directed to the sole end of establishing the possibility
and priority of moral action as the exertion of individual
human will under the conditions of freedom. As early as his
inaugural dissertation, Kant described the functions of understanding as (a) critical, and (b) dogmatic; in the latter
function, the concepts of understanding "issue in some ex-
emplar, which is conceivable only by pure intellect, and is the
common measure of all other things as far as real." [19] In what
was perhaps his most mature work,[20] he subjected religion to
the determination of the moral imperative. The popular tradition that Kant's philosophy is a bulwark of the institution of
religion was developed in either ignorance or complete mis-
understanding of his critical analysis of religion. In fact, Kant
starts by defining religion as an unnecessary appendage of morality and ends with a critical reduction of alternatives which
clearly indicates that the establishment of a Church which will
perform any real moral function is not only impractical, but
literally impossible.

The fundamental imperative of morals is for Kant to be
found in the autonomous self-legislation of an individual,
private, human will. Nothing else is good but this individual
will, and it is the measure of all goodness. It was the impossibility of translating this subjectivity of authority into any

---

stood to be embodied in the institutional structure of society, but it makes no
sense at all if interests are described as dependent upon the initiating will of
an individual agent (Rudolf von Ihering, *Law as a Means to an End*, trans.
Isaac Husik [New York, 1921], esp. chap. iii).

19. *Kant's Inaugural Dissertation and Early Writings on Space* (1770), trans.
John Handyside (Chicago, 1929), p. 49.
20. *Religion within the Limits of Reason Alone* (1793), trans. T. M. Greene
and H. H. Hudson (Chicago, 1934).

kind of an order, or institution, of external relations that made Kant's description of religion somewhat less than consistent. These remarks concerning his difficulties with the correlation of a subjective imperative and an objective order are intended to introduce the fundamental problem of Kant's political and legal philosophy.

The *Rechtslehre* of the *Metaphysik der Sitten* does not represent the best of Kant's thought; his political philosophy as a whole is confused and uncertain, mainly because he insisted, with the tradition of the period, on attempting to maintain an identity of morals, reason, and law. The implication of such identity is, of course, that the same imperative must serve as the elemental ground of all these functions of man; but it is manifestly impossible to translate the subjectivity of the moral imperative into the objectivity necessary in order to provide real legal authority. We are concerned with this restricted aspect of Kant's thought as it bears on the problem of the imperative.[21]

Religion within the Limits of Reason Alone is perhaps the best single source from which to derive the implications of Kant's description of the imperative. In the first place, the work is a profound critical analysis; Paulsen says that it "is the last of Kant's great works written in the full vigor of his intellect." Mainly, however, it is in this work that Kant finally faced directly the question of the status of his subjective imperative in the institutional order of men in organized society. It is unfortunate that Kant did not exploit the insight he evidenced at that time when he turned his attention to the philosophy of law itself, for his remarks here on the relation of morals and law are more consistent than his later rationalizations.

The final end of man, according to Kant, is the realization of that degree of freedom which will make moral action possible. "To become *free*, 'to be freed from bondage under the

---

21. Caird thoroughly diagnosed the inconsistencies of Kant's political and legal positions in *The Critical Philosophy of Kant* (Glasgow, 1889), a classic analysis which now seems largely forgotten.

law of sin, to live for righteousness'—this is the highest prize
he can win."²² Such freedom is realizable only within the ordered organization of a commonwealth: "the state of lawless
external (brutish) freedom and independence from coercive
laws is a state of injustice and of war, each against each, which
a man *ought* to leave in order to enter into a politico-civil
state." ²³ Kant refines Hobbes's statement by adding "*est* status
belli," precluding any possible circumstance of temporary
peace in which freedom and morality would be possible. The
achievement of individual morality, therefore, is dependent
upon "the establishment and spread of a society whose task
and duty it is rationally to impress these laws in all their scope
upon the entire human race." ²⁴

The realization of such an ethical commonwealth, however,
is dependent in the strictest sense upon the prior establishment
of law and order in social organization.

> A union of men under merely moral laws . . . may be
> called an *ethical,* and so far as these laws are public, an
> *ethico-civil* (in contrast to a *juridico-civil*) society or an
> *ethical commonwealth.* It can exist in the midst of a poli-
> tical commonwealth and may even be made up of all its
> members; (indeed, unless it is based upon such a com-
> monwealth it can never be brought into existence by
> man). It has, however, a special and unique principle of
> union (virtue), and hence a form and constitution, which
> fundamentally distinguish it from the political common-
> wealth. At the same time there is a certain analogy be-
> tween them, regarded as two commonwealths, in view of
> which the former may also be called an *ethical state, i. e.,*
> a *kingdom* of virtue (of the good principle). The idea of
> such a state possesses a thoroughly well-grounded ob-
> jective reality in human reason (in man's duty to join
> such a state), even though, subjectively, we can never
> hope that man's good will will lead mankind to decide
> to work with unanimity towards this goal.²⁵

The civil state, under law, is a necessary condition for the

22. *Religion within the Limits of Reason Alone,* p. 85.
23. *Ibid.,* pp. 88-89.
24. *Ibid.,* p. 86.
25. *Ibid.*

attainment of an ethical state; such a state defines the possibilities of moral action for men on earth. In this respect, there is moral *implication* in the establishment of the civil state; the ultimate purpose for which such a state is established is to provide the conditions necessary to moral action by individuals. This condition is precisely the point upon which the prevailing confusion of legal and moral authority has centered. The establishment of a civil society of law and order is a *prior* necessity for the operation of moral freedom; thus the moral imperative could hardly serve as the imperative necessary for the maintenance of the civil society. In the absence of civil law which exhibits an authority capable of achieving a degree of peace and order in the external relations of men, the conditions simply do not prevail under which alone man can exercise the freedom which is necessary to the recognition of the moral imperative. Morality, then, literally requires a condition of freedom under law—not under moral law or natural law, but under civil law. The establishment of a civil commonwealth does not, of course, guarantee that men *will* in fact be moral; the civil or legal task is that of providing a necessary set of conditions.

> In an already existing political commonwealth all the political citizens, as such, are in an *ethical state of nature* and are entitled to remain therein; for it would be a contradiction *(in adjecto)* for the political commonwealth to compel its citizens to enter into an ethical commonwealth, since the very concept of the latter involves freedom from coercion. . . . But woe to the legislator who wishes to establish through force a polity directed to ethical ends! For in so doing he would not merely achieve the very opposite of an ethical polity but also undermine his political state and make it insecure. The citizen of the political commonwealth remains therefore, so far as its legislative function is concerned, completely free to enter with his fellow-citizens into an ethical union in addition to the political or to remain in this kind of state of nature, as he may wish.[26]

26. *Ibid.,* pp. 87-88.

Those who do enter freely into an ethical commonwealth "agree to limitations, namely to the condition that this constitution of the ethical commonwealth shall contain nothing which contradicts the duty of its members as *citizens of the state.*" It is important to note that Kant does not modify this relation of the civil and the moral even when the latter is given divine religious status:

> When a politico-civil law, itself not immoral, is opposed to what is held to be a divine statutory law, there are grounds for regarding the latter as spurious, since it contradicts a plain duty and since the notion that it is actually a divine command can never, by any empirical token, be accredited adequately enough to allow an otherwise established duty to be neglected on its account.[27]

Many of Kant's views that otherwise appear contradictory, if not incomprehensible, are clarified if we can accept the above as his most critically reasoned description of the relation of civil law to the realm of moral activity. There is no question that the distinction of law and morals rests upon an understanding of the source of the imperative, nor any doubt that the two require quite different kinds of jurisdiction and therefore neither can be reduced to the other.

> A *juridico-civil* (political) *state* is the relation of men to each other in which they all alike stand socially under *public juridical laws* (which are, as a class, laws of coercion). An *ethico-civil* state [*zustand,* condition] is that in which they are united under non-coercive laws, *i. e., laws of virtue alone.*[28]

The legal authority is one of coercion and therefore a *real* imperative. Kant did not satisfactorily explain the source of the legal imperative, but it is important to recognize that the most severe moralist in our philosophic tradition was forced to the admission that the possibility of moral action depends upon the maintenance of a legal imperative which is itself not equivalent to nor derivable from the principles of morals as dictated by reason and human will. Had this aspect of Kant's thinking

27. *Ibid.,* pp. 90-91 n.
28. *Ibid.,* p. 87.

been understood, the history of his contribution to legal theory might have been something quite different from what we know it to have been. No complete English translation of *Die Religion innerhalb der Grenzen der blossen Vernunft* was available until the 1934 edition used here. It is a pity that the half-dozen pages tucked away in this little-read work should have contained the most mature reflection of Kant on the relation of law and morals, however succinctly and inadequately it is there stated.

The end of the civil state, then, is the attainment of freedom for man; in this sense, it can be said that the civil state evidences a kind of secondary or potential moral purposiveness. The difficulty is that the right of freedom cannot exist, nor can it be claimed as a right, until the imperative of law is operative. Only the law can give us freedom, but it must be noted emphatically that in Kant's view this does not in any sense imply an identification of "is" and "ought," nor a Hegelian definition of freedom. Kant is prohibited, by the dependence of morals upon law, from any attempt to ground the authority of law rationally in a doctrine of natural rights.

> If an ethical commonwealth is to come into being, all single individuals must be subject to a public legislation, and all the laws which bind them must be capable of being regarded as commands of a common law-giver. Now if the commonwealth to be established is to be *juridical,* the mass of people uniting itself into a whole would itself have to be the law-giver (of constitutional laws), because legislation proceeds from the principle of *limiting the freedom of each to those conditions under which it can be consistent with the freedom of everyone else according to a common law,* and because, as a result, the general will sets up an external legal control.[29]

A footnote adds that the italicized portion of the above citation is "the principle of all external rights." This reference, however, is not to freedom, but to a principle of equality; the necessity of a principle of equality fundamental to Kant's doctrine of freedom is generally recognized. What is not always so ap-

29. *Ibid.,* p. 90.

parent is the further similarity between Kant and the Utilitarians. It is not merely a fortuitous relation, for both theories left unresolved the dilemma of the relation between the subjective moral imperative upon which they insisted and the objective political order which both recognized as necessary.[30] However, the establishment of a principle of equality as the ground of the authority of law would seem even more difficult than to base that authority on freedom; Mill, for example, experienced some very real difficulties in trying to adjust these two principles. In Kant's case, it seems reasonably clear that the principle of humanity or any principle of equality would be completely irrelevant to any pre-legal society or condition of man. Reference to natural rights will not escape this quandary, for in Kant's view we would have to say that if they are natural, they are not rights; if they are rights, they are not natural.

Kant was no sentimentalist in respect to the rational and moral potentialities of his fellow-men; he was realistically skeptical—albeit pious and humane of temper—that the majority of men would evidence either good will or good sense. How then did Kant propose to coerce men into that degree of order under law which is the necessary condition of moral existence? If a moral man forces another to be law-abiding in order to ensure the conditions of morality, is he then not using that person as a means? What Kant should have made clear was that moral axioms, principles, and postulates make sense only on the assumption of conditions maintained by a coercive legal imperative which is pre-moral in derivation. Kant is very muddled on this matter. He speaks derisively of the politician who legislates according to a rule of expediency; but, when he faces the problem of precisely how legal order is to be established where it does not now exist, as in his essay on international order, we find this very un-Kantian description of the political process:

30. See the development of this theme in T. V. Smith, *Beyond Conscience* (New York, 1934), esp. pp. 316-317.

For, if these maxims can only attain the end at which they
aim by being published, they must be in harmony with
the universal end of mankind, which is happiness; and to
be in sympathy with this (to make the people contented
with their lot) is the real business of politics.[31]

This quotation follows an argument by Kant to the effect that,
in order to ensure that politics is based on "right," publicity
of maxims is necessary. He proposes the following "principle
of public right": "All maxims which require publicity, in order that they may not fail to attain their end, are in agreement
both with right and politics."[32] This remark, taken with the
previous one, seems to imply that men will recognize a right
principle when they see one, and that if men do so accept a
principle, it is, for this reason, right. Must we then infer also
that if they do not accept a principle, it is not right? The only
possible explanation of such a view expressed by Kant would
be a reference to his uncritical faith in a crude teleology of
design. In an earlier section of the essay on *Perpetual Peace,*
he writes concerning the guarantee of that peace:

This guarantee is given by no less a power than the great
artist nature *(natura daedala rerum)* in whose mechanical
course is clearly exhibited a predetermined design to
make harmony spring from human discord, even against
the will of man. Now this design, although called Fate
when looked upon as the compelling force of a cause, the
laws of whose operation are unknown to us, is, when considered as the purpose manifested in the course of nature,
called Providence, as the deep-lying wisdom of a Higher
Cause, directing itself towards the ultimate practical end
of the human race and predetermining the course of
things with a view of its realisation.[33]

The teleological metaphysic implied here does indeed suggest the Hegelian identification of "is" and "ought," but in
his later construction of moral theory, and especially in the
Critique of Practical Reason, Kant carefully avoids such a

31. *Perpetual Peace* (1795), trans. M. Campbell Smith (London, 1917), p.
195.
32. *Ibid.*
33. *Ibid.,* pp. 143-144.

commitment in his specific description of teleological principles as pragmatic "as if" postulates, and thus establishes the final essential subjectivity of moral primacy.[34]

Having come thus far with Kant, we are in truth skirting very close to the domain of Hegel. Out of these alternatives, Hegel did indeed develop a ground for the legal imperative which claimed the objectivity that Kant could not realize; but in so doing, Hegel sacrificed all individuation, and the universality he achieved was so lacking in concreteness that it was hardly more than an abstract and largely meaningless assumption which never made contact with legal processes and hence never became the ground of a real imperative.[35] In some respects, Kant was an unfortunate figure in the development of Western thought, for he cast the problems of philosophy into a dilemma of psychological subjectivism from which we have not yet escaped. What Kant formulated is a moral anarchy, the ever-recurring blight of ethical theory since his time. Although he insisted that "any legal constitution whatsoever, even although it conforms only slightly with the spirit of law is better than none at all," [36] yet the only imperative he ever described was the subjective, private, particular disposition of the individual will.

Political and legal thought of our recent past has concentrated attention on the perfection of the private, individual will. We have attempted to convert men to an obedience of law by preachment and moral suasion, whereas Kant made it perfectly clear that moral action was dependent upon the prior establishment of legal order. The legal imperative cannot be grounded in morals. We make an occasional gesture toward this analytic fact, but it is little more than a gesture. Our legal processes still proceed on premises somewhat as follows: if a man is possessed of enough intelligence that he cannot be ad-

34. See *The Philosophy of As If*, by Hans Vaihinger (New York, 1924).
35. British Hegelians worked on the problem with questionable results, as, for example, Bradley's painstaking effort to establish the nature of the "concrete universal."
36. *Perpetual Peace*, p. 168 n.

judged insane, then he knows the difference between right and wrong; he therefore knows that it is wrong to violate the law, and he knows what the law is, or he ought to; therefore, if he violated the law, it must have been the act of a bad or malicious will, and he is therefore individually responsible for his act. The law thus prosecutes and executes for an act of bad will; in this respect, it is not legal prosecution, but moral persecution.

The relationship of the necessary fact of legal enforcement and the desirable choice of moral judgment is left unclear and unspecified, confused in analysis and in language. Subsequent philosophic thought seems to have embalmed rather than clarified the confusion, and this has resulted in a critical controversy in respect to the limits of application, effectiveness, and enforcement of the criminal law which has generally been deemed essential to the preservation of the very fabric of social and political structure. On the one hand, we are told by able and forceful proponents that the social fabric is fundamentally and essentially moral and that the function of law is to maintain and safeguard that moral system, else the whole political structure will be endangered. On the other hand, a pendulum-like reaction to this moralistic interpretation of the law has approached the position of demanding total abrogation of the penal function of criminal law in a substitution of psychiatric analysis and sociological theory for the punishment normally considered necessary for the enforcement of law. In practice, the indictment is thus withdrawn from the criminal and brought against society; individual responsibility is disclaimed, and the whole meaning of law is placed in serious question, if not disrepute. While one may deplore the development of the "no bad boys" view into an effective forensic technique, it must be admitted that this is just what could be expected to result from juristic theory and practice which asserts the equivalence of legal liability and moral judgment.

The controversy is by no means idle, nor is it simply theoretical. A particularly forthright and vigorous statement of the moral interpretation of criminal law, for example, was recently asserted by Mr. Justice Devlin, Lord of Appeal in Ordinary.[37] His remarks were directed to the philosophy expressed in the Wolfenden Report, which was concerned with the question of whether homosexuality and prostitution should come within the purview of the criminal law. Justice Devlin states his definition of the social fabric: "What makes a society of any sort is community of ideas, not only political ideas but also ideas about the way its members should behave and govern their lives; these latter ideas are its morals."[38] At once, it must be suggested that this is not a definition of social structure, but of a very special kind of society. Kant properly recognized that *within* the political community there *might* also exist a community of moral ideas and that such moral agreement *might* lead to religious community. The requirement that the membership of these three communities that do, in fact, exist in all modern states must be co-terminous and mutually inclusive is a most unrealistic and unwarranted demand. Yet this is precisely what Justice Devlin does demand. Thus he claims: "It must be remembered also that although there is much immorality that is not punished by the law, there is none that is condoned by the law."[39] It would be very odd indeed if the criminal law as we know it were designed to approve either moral or immoral behavior; that is not the function of law. What is significant is the permissive latitude for moral or immoral behavior under the law: the possibility of endless lying short of contract, the infliction of misery short of assault, the drinking of intoxicating liquor short of drunkenness—and a host of actions which would be deemed wrong and sinful in *some* moral system.

In any such view as that presented by Justice Devlin, the inescapable question arises: *What* moral system should the criminal law enforce, and who decides this?

37. Sir Patrick Devlin, "The Enforcement of Morals," in *Proceedings of the British Academy*, 1959 (London, 1960), pp. 129-151.
38. *Ibid.*, p. 196.
39. *Ibid.*, p. 135.

It is that of the reasonable man. He is not to be confused with the rational man. He is not expected to reason about anything and his judgment may be largely a matter of feeling. It is the viewpoint of the man on the street ... the man in the jury box . . . principles which every right-minded person would accept as valid.[40]

As for *what* man on *what* street, and *what* man in *what* jury box, that must by now be self-evident; Justice Devlin quotes with approval Pollock's description: "A certain way of thinking on questions of morality which we expect to find in a reasonable civilized man or a reasonable Englishman, taken at random." It follows, of course, that this "reasonable Englishman" will be a "Christian" and will adhere to the moral system entailed by that religious commitment.

So the law must base itself on Christian morals and to the limit of its ability enforce them, not simply because they are the morals of most of us, nor simply because they are the morals which are taught by the established Church ... for the compelling reason that without the help of Christian teaching the law will fail.[41]

The employment of criminal law to enforce a particular set of moral precepts derived from a particular religious commitment is now established, and those persons who are not right-minded, Christian, and English will simply have to accept the imposition. "It seems to me therefore that the free-thinker and the non-Christian can accept, without offense to his convictions, the fact that Christian morals are the basis of the criminal law." [42] It is questionable whether, and in what way, such a description of the use of law is preferable to the undisguised appropriation of legal processes by sheer force in a bid for political power. The implications of this moralistic and sacerdotal definition of law are clear enough in their impact on the maintenance of orderly relations in a modern state comprising wide ranges of moral and religious belief. How much more damning are the results when such a view is brought into the

40. *Ibid.*, pp. 141-142.
41. *Ibid.*, p. 151.
42. *Ibid.*, p. 149.

courts of inter-national, inter-moral, and inter-religious arbi-
tration. Must we continue to present the philosophy of democratic political procedures as the only method for the realization of the justifiable end of government, the moral status of
persons, in terms which demand a prior commitment to a
particular set of theological precepts? Is this not an affront to
the sense and sensibility of reasonable men? One may express
profound dissatisfaction with the political and legal system of,
for example, Marxist-Soviet philosophy without professing a
belief in Christian religion, or any religion whatever. On the
contrary, profession of belief in the Christian religion does not
preclude an acceptance of Marxist philosophy.[43]

It is with sincere relief that we can observe directions of
thought which do not grasp and belabor either of these rationally untenable extremes of invoking the law to enforce moral
dicta or abrogating responsibility entirely. Not much help in
this development has come from the analysis of recent philosophy, but contemporary legal and juristic writing gives evidence of real progress toward the statement of a philosophy
adequate to the legal-moral context of man in a modern state.
One of the most perceptive of such treatments is that of Henry
M. Hart, Jr. in an article on "The Aims of the Criminal
Law." [44] Here we find a description of law which makes sense
of its function in maintaining social structure.

> The commands of the criminal law are commands which
> the public interest requires people to comply with. . . .
> Man is a social animal, and the function of law is to en-
> able him to realize his potentialities as a human being

43. See, e.g., the numerous works of John Lewis, especially *A Faith to Live
By* (New York, 1931); *Christianity and the Social Crisis* (London, 1935); *Marxism and Modern Idealism* (London, 1944); *Marxism and the Open Mind* (London, 1957).
44. *Law and Contemporary Problems*, XXIII (1958), 401-441.
Attention should be called to the profound treatment of this subject by Professor H. L. A. Hart ("Positivism and the Separation of Law and Morals") and
Professor Lon L. Fuller ("Positivism and Fidelity to Law—A Reply to Professor Hart"), reprinted from the *Harvard Law Review* (1958) in *Society, Law,
and Morality*, ed. F. A. Olafson (New York, 1961), pp. 439-505. These two
articles present such a detailed and mutually presumptive analysis that quotation short of almost complete reproduction would do violence to the logic and
symmetry of the discussion.

through the forms and modes of social organization. It is important to consider how the criminal law serves this ultimate end.

Human beings, of course, realize their potentialities in part through enjoyment of the various satisfactions of human life, both tangible and intangible, which existing social resources and their own individual capacities make available to them. Yet, the social resources of the moment are always limited, and human capacities for enjoyment are limited also. Social resources for providing the satisfactions of life and human capacities for enjoying them, however, are always susceptible of enlargement, so far as we know, without eventual limit. Man realizes his potentialities most significantly in the very process of developing these resources and capacities—by making himself a functioning and participating member of his community, contributing to it as well as drawing from it. . . .[45]

This ultimate end, it may be added, is the justifiable end of all law. The entailment of individual responsibility which follows from this description of the end of law is clear in respect to the employment of sanctions and enforcement.

Seen in this light, the criminal law has an obviously significant and, indeed, a fundamental role to play in the effort to create the good society. . . .

The core of a sound penal code in any view of the function of the criminal law is the statement of those minimum obligations of conduct which the conditions of community life impose upon every participating member if community life is to be maintained and to prosper. . . .

The inculcation of a sense of social responsibility throughout the society will be the dominant aim. But the stated obligations will, at the same time, represent desired standards of conduct and so will necessarily involve the aim of deterrence of undesired conduct. Since violators are to be condemned as defaulters in their duty to the community and treated accordingly, the aim can also be described as punitive.[46]

Professor Hart continues with an extensive analysis of the problems of realizing this philosophy in practical legal procedure, an area outside our present interest. The only negative

45. H. M. Hart, *op. cit.*, pp. 408-410.
46. *Ibid.*, pp. 410-413.

comment to be made on his statement is, I believe, a semantic observation. Occasionally he uses "moral condemnation" as if it were synonymous with what he properly terms "social" or "legal" condemnation. It seems clear from his definition of the criteria of law that he cannot mean that it is to be subjected to moral assessment as Kant defined moral, or as we have used it here. What Professor Hart says is that assessment of the law is a judgment of the extent to which it permits man to realize his potentialities and provides him the conditions for achievement of moral status. Law is not judged by its conformity to a particular moral code, and some of the confusion about this relationship could be avoided by more precise language than "moral condemnation"; such expressions allow moralistic proponents to ignore the essential significance of such analyses as that of Professor Hart and, by taking advantage of the linguistic ambiguity, to find in the statement an implication quite contrary to its meaning.

It would be inappropriate here to explore further the theory of criminal law. However, it would be negligent to leave the subject without mention of the most sustained and systematic contemporary effort to establish and define individual responsibility, and to distinguish legal liability from moral judgment —the distinguished and scholarly work of Jerome Hall.[47] In passing, it may be noted that Professor Hall takes a characteristic "no-nonsense" view of the proposals to eliminate sanction, punishment, and enforcement as ingredients of the law. He suggests sarcastically that, on this view, we are asked to say to the criminal: "We shall send you not to jail, but to Yale, our only regret being that attendance is compulsory." In a succinct analysis, he probes one of the aspects of this confusion of legal and moral:

> A legal system includes commands and sanctions; and the distinctive sanction of penal law is punishment—that sanction is the index of the kind of system or legal order that the criminal law is. Accordingly, since punishment

47. See especially *Living Law of Democratic Society* (Indianapolis, 1949), *Comparative Law and Social Theory* (Baton Rouge, La., 1963).

cannot validly be isolated from the concepts that give it meaning and since they, in turn, have no other purpose than that of sustaining punishment, the actual issue raised in the proposal for a treatment-board is abandonment of the criminal law.

If that should ever happen, the question now asked—what is criminal conduct or who are criminals, what harms must they have committed, what may be done to them?—would become literally "nonsense." But since men would not simultaneously be transformed into angels, the problems of harm-doing would persist.[48]

[III]

The continued description of legal accountability in terms of subjective moral perception has led to another problem of liability and punishment which is in some respects more critical than that of assessing individual responsibility in criminal law. The most strenuous advocate of "treatment and rehabilitation" would hardly argue that the criminal be accorded a status outside the jurisdiction of law. Yet a kind of irresponsibility which would not be countenanced in criminal law has been permitted in the wide area of action which comprises corporate enterprise. An individual will be quickly and forcibly apprehended and punished for theft or embezzlement, but a board of directors acting as a corporate body may embezzle with impunity in the form of stock option purchases and retirement consultantships; utilize corporate funds for vacations, airplanes, yachts; and indulge in other forms of swindling which shame the exploits of an ordinary, unincorporated criminal. However, the advantages of incorporation are now so obvious that criminals have increasingly availed themselves of this opportunity to become legally untouchable by organizing as a corporate business enterprise or labor union.

48. "The Purposes of a System for the Administration of Criminal Justice," a lecture delivered at Georgetown University Law Center, October 9, 1963, pp. 6-7. See also: "The Scientific and Humane Study of Criminal Law," *Boston University Law Review*, Vol. XLII, No. 3 (1962), pp. 267-281.

Because will has in our philosophy consistently carried a connotation of subjectivity, Anglo-American jurisprudence has never been able to take cognizance of the increasingly dominant fact of corporate will. Here is an action which is manifestly not the outcome of a freely electing subjective, individual will. Since our legal theory is not prepared to give credence to any act of will which is not resident in an isolable, particular individual, the legal process has found it difficult to analyze and judge corporate acts. The result is that the most egregious and outrageous violations of law are accomplished with impunity when the action is performed in a corporate capacity. If the individuals involved are careful to avoid the personal violations of non-payment of taxes or contempt, there is hardly any limit to the number of "corporate" crimes which can be committed without fear of personal punishment. Legal incorporation is the modern accomplishment of legal anarchy.

Anglo-American legal theory has thus admitted surreptitiously through the back door what was so ostentatiously thrown out the front. Our legal system has developed gradually a permissive irresponsibility of corporate bodies because action, responsibility, will, and duty have been consistently defined in terms of subjective motivation. The result has given rise to a paradoxical situation in which the law can deal adequately with an individual only if he is assumed to be in a "state of nature"—as we know he is not; the law cannot understand the individual as a member of the manifold corporate bodies which constitute legally ordered society—as we know he is. A parallel paradox is observable in those legal systems which have developed from the Hegelian substitution of abstract corporeity for Kantian subjectivism. The essential truth of Hobbes and Kant—that the legal ordering of society is for the purpose of making individual, moral action possible—is ignored in the failure to define the abstract universality of corporeity in concrete terms of individuation. The individual is not moral in such a system because there is, in fact, no individual left who possesses the characteristics necessary to constitute moral action.

Thus, under the legal system derived from Kantian subjectivism, the individual is held responsible for moral attitudes and actions within conditions of corporate circumstances which render moral action for the individual impossible. At the same time, circumstances of corporate order, the proper subject matter of law, have only with difficulty been brought within the purview of law because of the difficulty of adapting subjectivistic terminology and concepts to objective or corporate fact. On the other hand, those legal systems deriving from Hegelian objectivism, including the Marxist, relieve individuals of responsibility on the ground of corporate determination, even when it is clear that the corporate order in question does not fulfil the function of law in providing the conditions necessary for individual moral action. Under such a system, it is manifestly difficult to take account of the factors of individual will and determination which alone constitute agency in any real sense of the term. In the first instance, the law deals blindly with individuals; in the second, law perpetuates empty institutions. Both systems are left the easy prey of that ever-present substitute for rational authority and imperative: sheer power.

The question of individual liability for corporate action was the most debatable issue in all the so-called war criminal trials. That the problem was clarified in these prosecutions is doubtful. References to international law and the family of nations echo rather hollowly. The arguments in these trials present a confusing admixture of legal terminology and citation, enforced by moral righteousness and proclaimed with the authority of a military victor. Morally, the defendants were "guilty," but since we stopped burning witches, we claim not to stomach moral persecution. It has been argued, and not without reason, that these trials represented convictions by a military tribunal; an odor of moral retribution made the executions palatable to English and American sensibilities which would have cringed at sheer summary execution. Legal theory is reduced to sheer absurdity when it is argued that "although a soldier, in killing an enemy soldier, is for obvious reasons usually exempt from responsibility for murder, this rule of exemption nevertheless requires that the killing, even if done in warfare, be lawful."[49] This seems to require that an individual be illegal in a legal manner. *Silent leges inter arma.*

Moral aspirations may be commended, but, however inspiring, they do not alter the essential futility of procedures which assume that moral conviction will prove an adequate substitute for a legal imperative. Glueck, in the work cited above, seethes with moral indignation, for which most of us feel the deepest sympathy.

> It would be a heartening demonstration of a long overdue international firmness of purpose to maintain the people's peace through living law, if once and for all there were cast into the teeth of war-worshippers and war-mongers the cynical words of Field-Marshal-General Count von Moltke: "Perpetual peace is a dream, and it is not even a beautiful dream."[50]

Yet, how shall we then evaluate these ringing words of that most morally conscious of American jurists, Holmes?

> But in the midst of doubt, in the collapse of creeds, there is one thing I do not doubt, that no man who lives in the same world with most of us can doubt, and that is that the faith is true and adorable which leads a soldier to throw away his life in obedience to a blindly accepted duty, in a cause which he little understands, in a plan of campaign of which he has no notion, under tactics of which he does not see the use. . . . War, when you are at it, is horrible and dull. It is only when time has passed that you see its message was divine. I hope it may be long before we are called again to sit at that master's feet. But some teacher of the kind we all need. . . . We need it everywhere and at all times.[51]

What better evidence could be adduced to document the ob-

49. Glueck, *op. cit.*, p. 105.
50. *Ibid.*, pp. 102-103.
51. *Speeches* (Boston, 1934), p. 59.

servation that the assumed correlation between moral conviction and legal authority is a myth? Similar moral convictions
may adjust satisfactorily to contrary legal systems; similar legal
systems may tolerate contrary moral convictions. Identity of
value structure, in other words, does not imply identity of
legal authority, and it is therefore impossible to argue that
differences of value structure necessarily imply conflicts of
legal authority. Moral authority cannot provide the imperative for legal authority, and whenever such a claim is made, it
means simply that moral conviction (whether it be dogma,
conscience, or belief) is parading in the ill-fitting guise of political command. Only on this premise can an examination of
the nature and source of civil law proceed.

[CHAPTER IV]

AUTHORITY AS
POLITICAL FACT

The attainment of the best constitution is likely to be impossible for the general run of states; and the good law-giver and the true statesman must therefore have their eyes open not only to what is absolutely best, but also to what is best in relation to actual conditions. . . . The student of politics should also learn to distinguish the laws which are absolutely best from those which are appropriate to each constitution.[1]

THE classical alternative to sheer authoritarian support of the legal imperative has been the doctrine of *consent*, as tempting a siren as ever lured the wishful hopes of man. A general and vague notion of consent appears to be the uncritical assumption of all political theories except the most blatantly authoritarian. The doctrine has assumed manifold shapes, from the naïve descriptions of society as a simple contractual relation to the ultra-sophisticated techniques of mass manipulation by effective propaganda symbols. In none of its forms, however, has the consent theory clarified the problem of the authority of law.[2] The theory has not escaped the confusion which characterizes inquiries concerning the ground of the legal imperative; the failure to distinguish moral action as de-

1. Aristotle, *Politics*, trans. E. Barker (Oxford, 1946), pp. 155-156.
2. "The doctrine of consent which enjoys such great popularity today is nevertheless very old. . . . We have an admirable statement of it as far back as twenty-five centuries ago in Plato's *Republic*—and one might add that it has been unsatisfactory for the same length of time" (William Ebenstein, *Modern Political Thought* [New York, 1954], pp. 33-34).

pendent upon prior conditions of social organization has been even more evident in political than in legal theory.

"Governments derive their just powers from the consent of the governed" is a moral, not a political, axiom; it places the moral cart as far ahead of the analytic horse as do those theories of law which try to find the basis of the imperative in moral rightness. The problem of justice is not a primitive question in political and legal analysis, but a very advanced and sophisticated one.[3] Before we can rationally discuss what constitutes a "just" exercise of power, we must have some clear idea of what power is, a question which is not so simple as it might appear. The implication is not, of course, that evaluation and its problems are secondary in importance or interest; what is meant is that proper evaluation can be undertaken only on the basis of an understanding of the facts and circumstances to which value—positive or negative—must be attached. Factual analysis precedes moral evaluation; to inject moral evaluations into the analysis of facts will inevitably preclude an adequate analysis of fact. He is a poor scientist indeed who foregoes his research in nuclear fission because he fears the consequences of the hydrogen bomb; he is likewise a poor citizen and deficient as a moral being if he evidences no concern for the use of his data. There has been a great amount of obfuscation in this matter of the distinction of factual analysis and moral evaluation, and much of it has emanated from philosophers. We have been told that all judgments are evaluative; this introduces a none too subtle ambiguity into the term "evaluation." We have, in many instances, belittled factual analysis; a kind of sinister delight is sometimes evident in demonstrations that science is vulnerable. But error in factual analysis is not error in evaluation. The statement that the earth is spherical in shape might someday be proved to be factually wrong; it is neither right nor wrong morally, nor would its correction, *as a statement of fact,* have moral connotation.

3. See the excellent critique, "Political Justification," by H. B. Acton, in *Contemporary British Philosophy* (London, 1956), pp. 21-45.

The continuing effort to discover a moral ground for the authority of law has resulted in a more or less complete disregard of the analysis of pertinent fact. Our knowledge of some of the factual configurations of the political and legal process is deplorably limited; while we profess extensive knowledge of the moral implications of law, what we are asserting seems rather a profession of prejudice. It is discouragingly evident that moral evaluations without benefit of factual analysis are as vaporous as clouds blown with every shift of the prevailing wind. The primary question is not whether an imperative of law that can be described as "just" derives from the consent of those to whom the law is addressed; the problem is whether *any* imperative of law derives from that consent. It can hardly be denied that the question of whether a law *can* manifest real authority in the face of an absence of consent is important to the description of law. The question of authority is one of factual analysis, and while it would be quixotic to assume that any analysis of such a complex fact as that of consent would result in a final, comprehensive description, an effort should be made to understand the facts. The dominance of a subjectivist attitude in the analysis of those doctrines most concerned with consent has contributed to the neglect of this important problem of description. Consent has been assumed to be a subjective process of election by an individual employing his private capacities. We have not really advanced beyond the assumption that consent is a contractual relationship between A (the individual) and B (the state or society) . We know this description is quite inadequate, but the particularistic terminology persists in the negative solution of assuming that consent is implied by the absence of objection, or, as it is sometimes expressed, silence is acquiescence. Consent is understood as the agreement of a numerical majority of particular individuals. That this is a wholly unrealistic concept of any kind of consent which operates to establish obedience to law, we know on the basis of factual analysis in psychology, politics, history, and law itself. Even the cynical relativists who describe the inculcation of obedience in terms of propaganda stimuli are involved in the same subjectivist pattern; their symbols are designed to influence subjective individuals, and the group or mass mind which they so blithely hope to manipulate is a collectivity of particulars. It is for this reason that the most astute of propagandists—and pollsters—are so often wrong; resultant attitudes may be contrary to expectation, despite the fact that subjective individuals as such may have been more or less correctly analyzed.

That some form of consent is a necessary element in the constitution of legal authority has been implicit in every rational discussion of political organization. Plato discovered that the matter was not so simple as to be resolved by the propagation of a "royal lie"; after his experience at Syracuse he manifested the petulant, self-righteous attitude of the moralist:

> And then when the laws have been established, everything depends upon the following point. If the stronger party shows itself even more eager than the conquered party to obey the laws, then everything will go well, happiness will abound, and all these evils will take their flight. On the contrary, if any one refuses to conform to these principles I have laid down, he need not appeal to me or to anyone else for support.[4]

Aristotle was more astute: "The sort of constitutional system which ought to be proposed is one which men can be easily induced, and will be readily able, to graft onto the system they already have." [5] It is true that extremist advocates of authoritarianism in law and politics have assumed the possibility of achieving consent by the simple application of force. Such authoritarians proclaim that they will treat discontent by "employing this force inexorably whenever it is rendered necessary" (Mussolini) , or that they will "shoot those who say such

4. Epistle VII, 337, *Studies in the Platonic Epistles*, by Glenn R. Morrow (Urbana, Ill., 1935).
5. *Op. cit.*, p. 156.

things" (Lenin). We need not anticipate further analysis of consent with the suggestion that such views are unrealistic, for the more comprehensive political views of these advocates of violence make it clear that they are speaking of recalcitrant minority opinion; they, too, assume that their leadership will be accepted by a sufficient majority to constitute an imperative consent.

A historical survey of variations in statement and acknowledgment of the element of consent in the composition of the legal imperative would be of doubtful value. In our own political philosophy, where consent has been elevated to a determining methodological principle, what actually constitutes consent is as little understood as it is in those orders which try to depreciate it; in fact, it is questionable whether the arrogation of consent to the fetish of a symbol has not resulted in less rather than more understanding of its real nature. Certainly, the notion which looks upon the law-maker as the personal proxy of every one of his individual constituents is about as unrealistic as any description could be, and it makes for some very unrealistic legislation.[6] Yet it is precisely according to such a theory of consent that we are now trying to erect a structure of international law, and we shall probably be terribly disappointed and disillusioned when the superstructure collapses for want of a solid foundation. Could any argument be more unconvincing than that the Nuremberg Trials were judgments "under an organic act which represents the wisdom, the sense of justice, and the will of nineteen governments, representing an overwhelming majority of all civilized people"?[7] Organic act? Will? Majority? This contemporary version of the consent doctrine of law is in no single substantial element different from the simple explanation of consent as a contractual relationship between and among individuals. Consent as

6. How can we otherwise account for the paradoxical increase in the veto power and the legislative control exercised by the executive in our "representative" government?

7. As quoted in chap. ii n. 26.

the ground of law is still being described in terms of "wills" and "majorities," and the resultant theory of law is as fallacious and empty as was the political theory which described social structures as resting upon individual contractual relations. Even on the assumption that "wills" are such simple entities that they can be determined and expressed as "majorities"—although they manifestly cannot, it is still a moot question whether such a majority of will-determinations would, in fact, contribute an imperative quality to the law which attempted to express the majority will.

The fundamental question raised by the consent-contract theory of the legal imperative is really quite simple; perhaps it is the very semantic simplicity of the problem which allows it to be by-passed by the tortuous convolutions in which descriptions of the nature of law are apt to become engrossed. It is most pertinent to inquire at the very outset what happens to a contractual relation of the consent variety when the will of the majority shifts or changes. A contract based on consent remains a contract only so long as there persists that kind and degree of consent which gave rise to the contractual relation in the first place. It makes no difference in this relationship whether the consent is that of two individuals, two parties of several members each, or two countries each comprising several million consent-participants. Such contractual relations are just as strong as, and not one bit stronger than, the consent on which they are based—and it is important to remember that this consent is described in terms of individuals, wills, and majorities. Such a collectivity, depending as it does on a precarious and shifting numerical balance, cannot in any sense be described as "organic." It is questionable whether it meets any of the qualifications of legal contract. Whether or not there is any such thing as an "organic will," it is quite apparent that such a will could not be the product of momentary juxtapositions of agreement in random collectivities of unstable subjectivities. Such a situation more precisely describes the nature of a mob, and if it is to be assumed that kaleidoscopic mob action represents organic will, then the term "organic" has very little meaning indeed. At any rate, it is clear that no combination, addition, or extraction of subjective wills can provide a substantial ground for the authority of law.

The persistent assumption that a mere collectivity of subjective, individual wills is productive of a "general" or "organic" or "corporate" will is perhaps the main source of confusion in the effort to describe political authority. Thus, we speak of the "sovereign will"; that this expression represented anything analogous to an individual will was not the case even when "sovereign" referred to a single individual, much less when the term refers to a collectivity of individuals. Just because of the difficulty of getting out of this framework of psychologically subjective terminology, it has been impossible for our legal theory to make any sense at all of such concepts as the "will" of a corporation. It is manifest that the action of a corporation is not simply the additive product of the individual wills of its directors, and most certainly not of its stockholders. Yet, in the absence of such a specifically designated individual will, the law finds it difficult, if not impossible, to assess responsibility. The assessment of responsibility within a corporate structure is the fundamental theoretical and philosophical problem at issue in the war-criminal trials and in all efforts to declare the waging of aggressive warfare a crime. That our juristic theory was not prepared to cope with this problem has long been evident in the failure to define and establish guilt within the comparatively narrow limits of corporate administration.

It is somewhat surprising that the philosopher who was the primary source of this individualistic tradition in Anglo-American legal thought should himself have been much clearer on this matter of will than his successors and disciples. If this assertion seems dubious, it is to be explained by the fact that only comparatively recently has there been made available the manuscript in which Jeremy Bentham clarified his thought on the nature and source of law.[8] In this sequel to *An Introduction to the Principles of Morals and Legislation,* Bentham came very close to a formulation of the problem which continues to beset legal theory and which was derived mainly from his individualistic analysis. Bentham was honest in his thinking, if somewhat tortuous, and in this later work he evidences an awareness of the impossibility of finding an adequate ground for the authority of law in the characteristics of the subjective individual. Because of the unedited and unfinished nature of the manuscripts which make up the volume, this development of Bentham's thought is not apparent on casual reading, but there appears every reason to suppose that Bentham was quite well aware of what he was saying, and his notations in the manuscript often indicate his recognition that further development was needed.

There is no suggestion that Bentham changed his fundamental views in respect to the nature of the subjective individual as motivated by pleasure and pain, and this essential nature of man's motivation made it necessary that law in its penal aspect be directed to the individual as an *agent* who could be influenced through his capacity to suffer. The law relies for its effectiveness upon two motives: the "alluring" and the "coercive." Bentham admits that the preponderance of laws will derive their effectiveness from the latter motive. All civil law is penal law, for when the law defines an offense, it implies a punishment.[9] An offense can be defined only in terms of an act, and the only agent of action is a person. "The objects of

8. *The Limits of Jurisprudence Defined,* ed. C. W. Everett (New York, 1945). Professor Everett merits the gratitude of legal and philosophical scholarship for his discovery of this most important addition to the available corpus of Bentham's work. As editor, his restraint was praiseworthy in resisting what must have been a temptation to edit and correct this fragmentary and unfinished material. Unfortunately, the book does not seem to have received the attention it deserves; certainly no future comment on Bentham's legal and political philosophy can be considered competent if it does not take this material into account.

9. *Ibid.,* p. 53.

the laws are *acts*: yet no acts of any beings whatsoever but those of human beings only who are styled *persons*. The commencement then of every act must at any rate be in a person." [10]

The necessity of penal provisions in the law, then, imposes a limitation on the concept "person" as denoting only a human individual. Bentham did not deny the factual existence of institutions or their importance to the legal process, as we shall shortly see, but he did confine legal *agency* to the action of a describable individual. What he is defining, then, is a *legal* person.

> Coercion if it attaches at all can attach only upon individuals. Benefit men may receive from the law in their collective capacity: but it is in their individual capacities that it is addressed to them: if proved to have been transgressed it is by individuals that it must be proved to have been transgressed; if punished it is upon individuals that it must be punished.[11]

Now the penal provision is an essential and necessary element of every law whatsoever; it is, indeed, the factor of punishment which distinguishes private ethics from jurisprudence. Having treated of ethics in *An Introduction to the Principles of Morals and Legislation,* Bentham begins his discussion of jurisprudence with an initial emphasis on the penal aspect of law:

> We come now to speak of what is called civil law or jurisprudence on the one hand and penal law or jurisprudence on the other. . . . Between these two branches which are so often set in opposition to one another where lies the distinction? Nowhere. They are inextricably interwoven. What individual law is civil and not penal? There is no such thing. . . . without punishment, no such thing as law: without a motive no such thing as action.[12]

It seems rather clear, then, that if penal provision is a constituent element of every law and if provisions for punishment can be directed only toward individuals as such, it follows that individuals must be accepted as the units of all legal construc-

tion and process. The effect of this description of penal law is
to preclude the possibility that corporate entities as such can
be made proper objects of legal control or enforcement except
insofar as they can be controlled by controlling the actions of
individuals as agents.

Such an analysis is, of course, standard Benthamite doctrine,
the analysis which set the pattern and terminology of Anglo-
American juristic theory and practice. There is certainly no
question that Bentham meant to restrict agency to individuals
taken singly and separately, and he insisted that the enforcement of law must be accomplished by directly influencing the
motives of such individuals. The motives of individuals he
described generally as dominated by calculations of pleasure
and pain; motives are therefore capable of extensive description and classification, as all of Bentham's works indicate. The
question arises, then, whether Bentham's theory of jurisprudence ought not to describe a "legal calculus" which would in
effect enforce his "moral calculus." It is precisely this interpretation which seems to have become our implicit philosophy
of legal procedure, so that in some cases enforcement of the
law takes on the appearance of rather plain enforcement of
moral conviction.[13]

Now if the end and purpose of law were to make individual
persons into moral beings according to some preconceived
ethical pattern, the law would on Bentham's terms be just such
a legal calculus designed to enforce the moral calculus. That
this cannot be Bentham's meaning is clear from his many unrestrained attacks upon those who would legislate morals. In
the last chapter of *An Introduction to the Principles of Morals
and Legislation,* he discussed the distinction between "private

13. In a review of *The Limits of Jurisprudence Defined (Ethics,* July, 1945),
I indulged in this ready-made and traditional, but uncritical, extrapolation
from Bentham's moral calculus to a legal calculus representing his system of
jurisprudence. A more careful reading of what Bentham said in this later work,
and especially a consideration of the total context of his moral and legal philosophy, convinced me that this was a careless and erroneous interpretation of
what Bentham was about in this exploratory speculation on the source of the
imperative.

ethics" and "jurisprudence." Here he describes private ethics as the "art of self-government," and legislation as the "art of directing their actions . . . upon the principle of utility." The most general end of private ethics is happiness; the end of legislation is the same. "Thus far, then, private ethics and the art of legislation go hand in hand. The end they have, or ought to have, in view, is of the same nature."[14] Bentham recognizes that in society the happiness which is the end of private ethics cannot be dissociated from the happiness or well-being of the community. He does not, however, participate in the general fallacy of confusing a broad similarity of purpose with an identity of means.

Bentham is as disdainful as Kant of the legislator who would try to achieve moral action by coercion.

> It is only with respect to those broad lines of conduct in which all persons, or very large and permanent descriptions of persons, may be in a way to engage, that he can have any pretence for interfering; and even here the propriety of his interference will, in most instances, lie very open to dispute. At any rate, he must never expect to produce a perfect compliance by the mere force of the sanction of which he is himself the author. All he can hope to do, is to increase the efficacy of private ethics, by giving strength and direction to the influence of the moral sanction.[15]

In the light of our legislative experiments, it is interesting to note Bentham's selection of instances not subject to legislation.

> With what chance of success, for example, would a legislator go about to extirpate drunkenness and fornication by dint of legal punishment? Not all the tortures which ingenuity could invent would compass it: and, before he had made any progress worth regarding, such a mass of evil would be produced by the punishment, as would exceed, a thousandfold, the utmost mischief of the offence. The great difficulty would be in the procuring evidence; an object which could not be attempted, with any probability of success, without spreading dismay through every

14. (Oxford, 1879), p. 313.
15. Ibid., pp. 319-320.

family, tearing the bonds of sympathy asunder, and root-
ing out the influence of all the social motives. All that he
can do then, against offences of this nature, with any
prospect of advantage, in the way of direct legislation, is
to subject them, in cases of notoriety, to a slight censure,
so as thereby to cover them with a slight shade of artificial
disrepute.[16]

Bentham distinguishes the self-government of private ethics
as *prudence;* public virtues, comprising the duties toward
one's neighbors, he describes as *probity* and *beneficence.* Of
these, "the rules of *probity* are those, which in point of expediency stand most in need of assistance on the part of the
legislator."[17] Probity is defined as the negative discharge of
one's duties to his neighbors by forbearing to diminish the
happiness of others, comprehending a class of acts which can
be prohibited by law and for which compliance may be had
by coercion.[18] It is significant that Bentham did not include
either prudence or beneficence among the necessary qualifications of members of a proper electoral body, but rather *probity, intellectual aptitude,* and *active talent.*

It is very easy to overindulge the inclination to make a de-
fenseless author say what one wants to hear said; but it is also
quite proper, on the other hand, to point out implications of
what he says beyond his actual statements. In Bentham's case,
I believe, there is particular significance for the problem of
the imperative in what he implied but did not clearly state.
It is ironic that Bentham should have to be charged with terminological carelessness, for it was on the subject of classification, description, and terminology that Bentham could be
most eloquent and caustic. Some of this confusion undoubt-

16. *Ibid.,* p. 320.
17. *Ibid.,* p. 321.
18. Bentham properly places *beneficence* within the area of private ethics
because it involves a subjective determination of "conduct free and voluntary";
but he suggests that the law could be extended under this head. However, the
examples he cites are, by his own definition, clearly instances of the enforcement of probity: "A woman's head-dress catches fire: water is at hand: a man,
instead of assisting to quench the fire, looks on, and laughs at it" (*ibid.,* p.
323 n. 1). Cf. the statement in *The Theory of Legislation,* ed. C. K. Ogden
(London, 1931), chap. xii.

edly results from the rather haphazard form in which much of his work has come to us; but, with all qualifications admitted, there is still evident a regrettable looseness of reference in some of the most fundamental concepts employed by him. However, we are not here primarily interested in what he meant to say or would have said, but in the implications of his descriptive explorations for the analysis of political fact.

Without doing violence to Bentham's thought, then, it appears that we may say that legislation is the enforcement of those rules of conduct in the relations of men which must be maintained in order to ensure the possibility of happiness for each man. As did Kant, Bentham describes a condition of civil law as a necessary condition of morality, and he agrees with Kant that law is limited to the provision of these conditions; law cannot enforce morality, but only provide the conditions for morality. The function of civil government, therefore, is the establishment of an orderly and peaceful organization of those material circumstances of existence which, if ordered, will enable men to exercise the intelligence and volition essential to moral action. Bentham describes these material circumstances, which are the "ends of civil law," as Subsistence, Abunance, Equality, and Security.[19] By equality he expressly means "the distribution of property."

When we ask what the motives are which dispose men to accept the state of civil law, Bentham is less clear in his analysis. At one point, he ignores the question with the comment that the fact of the establishment of government he assumes "as notorious, and the necessity of it as alike obvious and incontestable."[20] He repeatedly asserts that "the only interests which a man at all times and upon all occasions is sure to find *adequate* motives for consulting, are his own." He tempers this, however, with the qualification that "there are no occasions in which a man has not some motives for consulting the happiness of other men." Bentham here explains these motives

19. *Theory of Legislation*, pp. 96-97.
20. *An Introduction to the Principles of Morals and Legislation*, p. 214 n. 1.

by reference to sympathy, benevolence, love of amity, and love of reputation.[21] Even if one could believe that Bentham was sufficiently optimistic about his fellow men to believe that a majority of them would evidence such public virtues, they would still not provide the motives of that disposition which is required as the ground of the legal imperative.

The inadequacy of virtues, private or public, as the source of political authority becomes evident when Bentham comes to consider more precisely the grounds of legal enforceability. Law is directed to individuals, and it is therefore upon the influence of individual motives that the enforcement of the law depends. The only justification which Bentham will allow for any law is the "promotion of the public good," the greatest happiness of the greatest number. The end of law, thus defined, is for Bentham the undeniable dictate of the "principle of utility." It distorts the whole structure of Bentham's thought if it is not recognized that for him utility was a factual principle, derived from an observation and description of the facts of individual motivation and social organization under law. To interpret the greatest good of the greatest number, the maximum satisfaction of individuals within the social structure, as a moral argument is to make meaningless much of Bentham's construction from the principle of utility. He did not say that "the greatest good of the whole community" *ought* to be the ultimate end of law; he said: "As to the general and ultimate end, this upon the principle of utility can be no other, than the greatest good of the whole community."[22] The end of law *can* be no other. It is sometimes forgotten that Bentham was not sentimental about democracy and did not base his arguments for representative processes on moral

21. *Ibid.,* p. 313.
22. *The Limits of Jurisprudence Defined,* p. 113. As for the principle of utility, Bentham says, "This then I assume as a *postulatum*. If it be denied me, I confess that I shall be altogether at a loss to prove it" (p. 116). Here is introduced a nice point of discrimination in respect to value theory: whether such a *postulatum* is itself a value judgment. I do not think that it is, unless we are to admit that *all* judgments are value judgments. This is an important problem, but I do not think it materially affects what Bentham has to say about the factual nature of the legal imperative. See below, chap. vi.

grounds. It seems, rather, that he came to accept democracy
with all its implications as the only social method which could
be justified on utilitarian grounds.[23] Thus, Bentham considered the exercise of legal enforcement to be severely limited
in respect to such matters as coinage and weights and measures;
arbitrariness in such areas, he argued, would foment revolution.[24]

What Bentham is saying, then, is that while the law must
be directed to men in their individual capacities, and while
any single law can be justified only if it adds to the sum total
of happiness in the community, yet neither of these criteria
adds much to our understanding of the source or ground of
the necessary imperative of the law. The first requirement is
methodological, similar to Bentham's strong insistence upon
the clear, written presentation of laws in codified form. The
law must be communicated to individuals because individuals
are the only agents, and hence the units of obedience and disobedience. The second requirement is the necessary addition
of a value criterion in order that law may be able to justify its
penal provisions. Bentham was more perceptive than Kant on
this point; for, if free moral action is the ultimate rational
demand made upon men, then certainly any law of compulsion must exhibit a reason for its apparent limitation of freedom through exercise of the imperative. Bentham insists upon
such an evaluative justification of law:

> No restraint should be imposed, no power conferred, no
> coercive law sanctioned, without a specific and satisfac-
> tory reason. There is always one reason against every
> coercive law, and one reason which, were there no other,
> would be sufficient by itself: it is, that such a law is re-
> strictive of liberty.[25]

The individual is also the unit of evaluative judgment; the
"greatest good of the greatest number," which is the generic

23. On this point, see E. Halevy, *The Growth of Philosophic Radicalism*,
trans. M. Morris (New York, 1928), esp. Pt. II, chap. i.
24. *The Limits of Jurisprudence Defined*, p. 174.
25. *The Works of Jeremy Bentham*, ed. Sir John Bowring (Edinburgh, 1838-
1843), I, 301.

criterion for evaluating the law, is not for Bentham an esoteric, amorphous norm. It is the product of individual goods, and evaluation is made by individuals, consulting their own motives and happiness. Individuals do indeed take account of the motives and happiness of others, but only as a necessary circumstance of social communication.

This elaborate structure of methodology and value criterion does not, however, describe law, and Bentham knows it. Neither method nor individual value discrimination provides the source of that imperative which alone enables the law to compel obedience. If Bentham's description were confined to these two elements, he would indeed not have described law at all, but merely have elaborated the pattern of moral motivation and evaluation. In this case, the only justifiable exercise of punishment would be that visited by an individual upon himself, a description of legal anarchy. Throughout *The Limits of Jurisprudence Defined* there is constantly recurring evidence that Bentham recognized this problem and intended to explore the factual grounds for the "power of imperation"; he seems well aware that thus far he had simply assumed the existence of this power. Certainly, Bentham was not of the opinion that value structure would of itself provide a source of legal power of imperation, and just as certainly did he refuse to believe that law was nothing more than a positivistic monopoly of force. One of his comments on the limitation of power has already been remarked; on this point he is even more specific:

> At any rate it appears that the power of the legislator and the power of the despot are not even when put together equal to the whole power of imperation in the state: that a chasm is still left, to supply which requires the addition of the several modifications of power which may be included under the names of accensitive and disaccensitive.[26]

The "accensitive" power had already been discussed in the chapter of which the above quotation is the conclusion, but

26. *The Limits of Jurisprudence Defined*, p. 176.

that Bentham was not satisfied is indicated by his note to himself at the end of the chapter: "Go on with the distinction between the power of accensation etc. in classes and in singulis and singula."[27] Again, in a later chapter, after he has remarked that the legislator must command but cannot take upon himself the infliction of punishment because "he would be overstepping the bounds of his own function and exercising a different sort of power," Bentham has again written himself a note: "Work this up with the rest of what concerns imperation under title Generality."[28] The title "Generality" refers to the chapter containing the quotation and note on accensitive power cited above.

In a rather awkward manner Bentham has formulated the problem of the authority of law more precisely than is generally recognized by the jurisprudence which derives its basic concepts from his thought. Bentham described the method and evaluation of law in terms of individual motivation and evaluation, but he realized that neither motivation of pleasure-pain nor the calculation of happiness provides the unitary source of power necessary to give law its imperative quality. In this advanced work Bentham begins to see that the mere assumption of "government," or of "sovereignty," is a tour de force answer to the question of what constitutes the power of imperation. True, if account is not taken of Bentham's dissatisfaction, and particularly of the manifestly unfinished state of both his manuscript and his thinking, it might appear that he resolves the question of imperation by a simple extension of his pattern of individualistic analysis. Thus, when he discusses the source of a law, he asserts that it must be an expression of the "will of the sovereign in a state."[29] That he is not content, however, to accept the classic assumption of sovereignty is indicated by his effort to state more specifically what he means by this power:

27. *Ibid.*, p. 177.
28. *Ibid.*, p. 228 and n.
29. *Ibid.*, p. 101.

Now by a sovereign I mean any person or assemblage of persons to whose will a whole political community are (no matter on what account) supposed to be in a disposition to pay obedience: and that in preference to the will of any other person.[30]

The qualifications of "no matter on what account" and "supposed to be" are an indication of Bentham's uncertainty, but in other passages he unqualifiedly establishes the imperative in "disposition" to obedience.

The ultimate efficient cause of all power of imperation over persons is a disposition on the part of those persons to obey: the efficient cause then of the power of the sovereign is neither more nor less than the disposition to obedience on the part of the people.[31]

"The power of the governor is constituted by the obedience of the governed."[32] For Bentham, then, a law is a command which anticipates obedience on the part of those to whom it is directed; law serves as a stimulus to action in accord with an already existing disposition to act. The primary qualification of a legislator would seem to be knowledge of the disposition of the individuals to whom law is to be directed.[33]

Now at first glance it may appear that Bentham has treated us to a rather dizzy ride on a merry-go-round of analysis, for is this final resolution of the imperative in "disposition" not, in fact, a return to the old doctrine of consent in a rather naïve form? So it would seem, and so has Bentham been generally understood as establishing the enforceability of law on the consent of majorities of individuals. Perhaps this is indeed what he has said in his previously available works, but *The Limits of Jurisprudence Defined* makes it clear that he was not at all satisfied with his own description. He made a few very brief efforts to specify what he meant by "disposition," not very successful efforts as his manuscript notes indicate; his failure or inability to elaborate these preliminary suggestions

30. *Ibid.*
31. *Ibid.*, n.
32. *Ibid.*, p. 153.
33. Cf. above, p. 89.

was a truly great loss to modern juristic theory.[34] It would be a careless mistake to consider that Bentham's description of imperation was a mere resort to disposition dictated by an excess of zeal for subjectivistic analysis, that he simply insisted upon placing the entire burden of responsibility for imperation on the individual. If Bentham is guilty of reliance upon an undefined premise, then it must be admitted that every legal theory which is not blatantly authoritarian is equally guilty. Jurists less individualistically inclined than Bentham have also been forced to an admission of the high importance of the obedience of the governed to the essential structure of law. The admission sometimes takes the form of an assumption that recognition of the rational, natural, or divine character of law will automatically produce a disposition to obedience. The proof of the prevalence of the assumption, however, is the inability of any legal theory to maintain itself if a disposition to disobedience were to be assumed. Any effort so to establish law on a premise of disposition to disobedience would constitute a self-reduction, and the resultant description would be of a police state rather than of a legal system of order. The problem of the legal imperative is confused beyond resolution if this distinction of the disposition to obedience is not clearly recognized; while the importance of disposition seems to have been pretty generally admitted by assumption in legal speculation, Bentham is one of the few who have had the resolution to attempt a clarification of the premise.

The actual clarification which Bentham achieved is slight, and it will suffice for the moment to point out briefly the nature of his suggestion and what *might* have been developed from it. The description of disposition appears baffling because of the diversity and plurality of the manifestations of disposition, for, as Bentham remarks: "The obedience of the gov-

---

34. There still remain, in University College, London, some 173 portfolios, each containing about 600 pages of Bentham manuscript, in addition to the several volumes of papers and manuscript in the British Museum. Another "find" such as that of Everett is therefore quite possible, given a scholar sufficiently devoted to transcribe Bentham's almost indecipherable script.

erned is susceptible of every modification of which human conduct is susceptible: and the rules which mark it out, of every diversity which can be clearly described by words."[35] Yet, if disposition is to serve as the ground and source of imperation, it clearly must manifest the possibility of description in terms of some degree of coherence and continuity, but such does not seem to be the nature of disposition. "Now this disposition it is obvious may admit of innumerable modifications —and that even while it is constant; besides that it may change from day to day."[36] Bentham does not try to escape the difficulty by the trick of personalizing the concept of sovereignty. "The people may be disposed to obey the commands of one man against the world in relation to one sort of act, those of another man in relation to another sort of act."[37]

The impasse to which Bentham has brought himself cannot, of course, be resolved by asserting that law imposes order upon the dispositions which have already been defined as the source of the imperative of law. It is apparent that the nature and source of disposition itself must be explored, and to this exploration Bentham has given us a clue.

> By what means then can a law *in principem* be enforced and rendered efficacious: what force is there in the nature of things that is applicable to this purpose? To answer this question, we have nothing to do but to resort to the enumeration, that has already been given on a former occasion, of the several sorts of forces by which the human will is liable to be influenced. The forces and the only forces by which the human will is influenced are *motives*: these, when considered in the mass, may be distinguished according to the sources from whence they issue: to these sources we set out with giving the name of sanctions.[38]

Bentham's extensive treatment of "sanctions" is well-known; what is significant for our consideration of authority is the modification which Bentham feels constrained to make of his general view of sanctions when these are considered as means to the enforcement of law. "Of these sanctions that which we

35. *Ibid.*, p. 153.   37. *Ibid.*
36. *Ibid.*, p. 101.   38. *Ibid.*, pp. 151-152.

termed the *physical* is out of the question: for the force in the case in question is supposed to be directed by design."[39] Now this is indeed a curious statement for Bentham to make; surely he does not here mean to imply that the physical sanction is not an essential and calculable factor in the calculus of motivation. He has, in fact, said: "Of these four sanctions the physical is altogether, we may observe, the ground-work of the political and the moral: so it is also of the religious, in as far as the latter bears relation to the present life."[40] Yet, as the source of authority becomes a more pressing question in his analysis, Bentham eliminates the physical sanction as a source of motivation which gives imperative force to law.[41]

There seems only one reasonable explanation for the selection of political, religious, and moral sanctions as representative of a ground for authority. In his brief and undeveloped remarks on these sanctions as the source of the imperative, Bentham is clearly implying some area of fact other than individual self-determination. The political, the religious, and the moral, as Bentham is now using them, are sanctions, are motivations, are the source of authority, because their force derives from a configuration of social fact which is essentially different from that of the individual.[42] It would seem that what Bentham is here calling the "moral" sanction could be more properly called *custom*. While he considered customary *law* altogether inferior to statutory law because of its uncertainty

39. *Ibid.*, p. 152.
40. *An Introduction to the Principles of Morals and Legislation*, p. 27.
41. Cf. *The Limits of Jurisprudence Defined*, p. 224.
42. In respect to this interpretation it is significant to note that in the *Fragment on Government* (1776) Bentham listed only three sanctions: political, moral, and religious. The "moral" seems not to be defined in terms of pleasure-pain, for Bentham prefers the term "popular." Four years later, when treating of ethics in *An Introduction to the Principles of Morals and Legislation*, he added the "physical" sanction. Apparently following the list in "Logical Arrangements" (*Works*, III, 290), Bowring in *Deontology* adds a fifth, the "social" or "sympathetic" sanction. In the *Principles*, Bentham had again remarked that the moral was "better termed *popular*, as more directly indicative of its constituent cause." Yet, he hesitated to use the expression "public opinion" because this sanction exerts influence only "through the medium of the affections and the will" (p. 25 n.).

and lack of precision, he nevertheless admitted the strong effect of custom as a sanction.

At present we may boldly affirm that among all the system [sic] of law which prevail among the several nations of the world, there is not one which does not exist more or less of it in the form of customary law: so that as yet no instance of a complete code of statute law is any where to be found. It follows not however by any means that if a complete code of that kind were given to any nation it must thereby be deprived of so much as a single article of those ancient and respected institutions to which the people in many instances with great reason are so strenuously attached.[43]

Such an interpretation of Bentham is the only view which makes sense by avoiding a manifest and flat contradiction. Unless sanctions are understood as the concrete manifestations of influence of *institutional* structures rather than described, on the contrary, as self-determined motivations of individuals, then the enforcement of law through manipulation of sanctions by the legislator is precisely the moral legislation of "the Elect" against which Bentham so vigorously declaimed. That Bentham should ever have departed so far from his fundamental convictions as to seek the ground of legal authority in moral principles or evaluations is impossible to believe. His only alternative would have been to examine the nature of social structure as it is manifested through institutional forms; whether he would then have found it necessary to include any sanctions other than the political, the religious, and the moral is a matter of speculative construction.[44]

The disposition to obedience, then, must be a concrete manifestation, in the form of individual motivation, of the force of institutional sanctions. Disposition of this nature is obviously a quite different kind of thing from the contract-consent, collectivity notion of social organization; disciples of Bentham have hardly done justice to the master. In modern philosophy two apparently opposing and contradictory analyses of social

43. *The Limits of Jurisprudence Defined*, p. 332.
44. As, for instance, an economic sanction; in *The Theory of Legislation* he defined equality as "the distribution of property" (p. 97 n.).

structure and legal authority are now seen as directional approaches to the same fundamental problem: *how do institutional sanctions become individuated in the form of motivations which influence individuals to action?* The point of view which has been argued in this discussion of the imperative is that the problem has been persistently confused by the failure to see what kind of a problem it is. The continuing effort to derive legal authority from a purported moral imperative is, as we have seen, an abortive procedure. In the first place, "moral imperative" is a concept which manifests an intrinsic contradiction; every moral imperative, so-called, must appeal to some source external to itself as the ground of its imperative quality, be that source called God, nature, reason, sex, or economics. Traditionally, the effort to find a suitable ground for the imperative quality of morals in order to support the derivation of legal authority has resulted in some very specious metaphysical postulations. We have noted, for instance, how even the rigorous Kant was driven to such questionable metaphysical support; that such a philosopher should indulge in the argument from design to the extent of asserting that it is a mark of Divine Providence that ocean currents carry driftwood to the shores of Iceland so that the natives there will have fuel for fire *(Perpetual Peace)* is an indication of the serious nature of the problem. Hegel accomplished the complete reduction of metaphysical support of the imperative by dogmatically asserting a set of metaphysical presuppositions which effectively did away with any distinction between moral judgment and political authority.

No one could sensibly deny that the problem of political authority is a facet of a larger whole of concern which includes moral and metaphysical speculation, a circumstance which would be equally true of problems in aesthetics, science, or epistemology. These broader implications of the problem of authority are not going to be clarified, however, until the essential structure of the imperative is understood. We cannot go on using such ambiguous terms as "disposition to obedience" and expect to arrive at any reasonable description of the imperative, when we clearly do not know what we mean by "disposition." It will remain difficult to understand *why* an individual is disposed to obey the law until it is more clearly understood *how* he is disposed.

CHAPTER V

POLITICAL FACT

*Most important of all, however, has been the gradual re-
alization of the difference between statements of fact and
judgments of value. A fact is a fact no matter what its
moral value may be. Nevertheless . . . human beings have
a tendency to deny something to be a fact when they do
not like it, or to affirm something to be a fact because that
is the way they would like things to be. . . . What is even
more confusing and equally illogical is the tendency to
assign moral value to a fact when that fact is per se completely innocent of such value.[1]*

THE intent of the preceding chapter was to show how Bentham suggested certain directions of speculation which
promise fruitful development of our general philosophy of
law. Released from confinement as the father of the Analytical
school, Bentham may again perhaps assume the stature he
merits in our tradition of juristic thought. In fact, the significant implication of this analysis of the disposition to obedience is that the traditional "schools" of legal philosophy have,
through deviously different channels, come out in the same
cul-de-sac. The value of Bentham's analysis, it seems to me, is
that it opens a path for further progress, while the definition
of authority in terms of some undefined *norm* presents an im-
ponderable which can be supported only by the assertion of a
metaphysical principle as arbitrary as the support of sheer
force itself. Pound has remarked that a choice is impossible "as
between the force theory and the consent theory and the
justice theory. . . . They represent elements in the law which

1. Marten ten Hoor, "Philosophers and Scientists Exchange Compliments,"
The Journal of the Alabama Academy of Science, XXV (1953), 5.

are in an irreducible antinomy, an ineradicable contradiction." So they have appeared; and while it is pleasantly optimistic to believe that as long as law "maintains a social order in which we may maintain and further civilization" there will be a "habit of obedience,"[2] this is little solace in the face of the hard fact that different institutional configurations induce different dispositions to obedience. As long as national sovereignties, claimants to political authority, represented particular institutional configurations, and as long as the task of law was largely confined to the establishment and maintenance of order *within* a particular configuration, a pattern of obedience could be assumed.[3] We mistakenly attributed the configuration of the disposition to obedience to a subjective majority agreement on moral principles and evaluations, whereas Bentham has suggested that the disposition which grounds legal authority must be defined in terms of the *facts* of the political, religious, economic, and other institutional components of the social structure. Moral action and discernment are the ends of law, not its source or ground. Until we are clear about the nature of that ground, moral discernment will remain haphazard. Until we understand that institutional structures are the ground of the disposition which alone provides the authority for any system of law, we can have no adequate philosophy from which to approach the critical problem of the mutual adjustment of systems of law which derive their authority from different systems of institutional structure.

Thus the heavy reliance throughout juristic speculation on something called "disposition" as the unavoidable ground of the necessary authority of law indicates that the nature of that authority is not going to be clarified until the nature of what is meant by disposition is more clearly understood. This problem is one of factual rather than legal analysis, and it has been

2. *Op. cit.*, pp. 53-54.
3. From a somewhat different point of view Peter Laslett argues convincingly that political theory has persisted in the use of a model, inherited from the Greeks, which is not appropriate to modern social structures: the model of a "face to face society" (*Philosophy, Politics and Society,* ed. Laslett [New York, 1956], chap. x).

greatly complicated because in almost every instance the disposition adduced by law has been equated with moral disposition. It is this tacit assumption, that the disposition evidenced by an individual must be a reflection of moral sentiment, which has forced specific legal theories to rely on specific theories of moral sentiment for authoritative support. The task, then, is to seek for an understanding of what is meant by disposition in the sense in which it has traditionally been used in this context.

The analysis of disposition is not, therefore, an investigation within the framework of legal theory, nor is it to be accomplished by an elucidation of moral sentiments or postulates. It is significant that moral theory has come up against the same apparently impenetrable barrier of disposition as has legal theory. Kant was greatly perplexed by the question of what to do with the individual who did not evidence a "good will" or disposition to good action (Kant here even uses "predisposition"—*Anlage*); his answer is not very enlightening to the moralist, much less to the exponent of legal imperation, for Kant said simply that the individual ought to be shown the example of men who do evidence "good will" in the hope that he will respond to their attitudes and actions. A more contemporary form of the surrender to inexplicable "disposition" is, of course, to be found in the Intuitionist moral view, where ignorance of the nature of disposition is deliberately arrogated to an arbitrary rule.

The nature of disposition is a problem which neither moral nor legal theory is prepared to elucidate, for such an analysis necessitates an examination which, if not more fundamental, is at least of a different order, and one which must normally provide the data for moral and legal construction. The vexing nature of this problem is that what we want to understand is the fundamental nature of an *act,* and while this definition ought to be a matter of factual description, it has not been so. When the pursuit of the problem of the ground of obedience to law, or that of the discrimination of moral choice, leads inevitably to an analysis of the act itself, we find that our observation is so hazy and blurred that the only recourse is to give a name to the unknown. If the name becomes popular and widely adopted, it is likely to precipitate a new "school" of philosophy.

Now if disposition in the individual is a resultant of the institutional configuration within which he acts, there is no reason why the nature of that disposition should remain mysterious. The structure and operation of institutions, and the influence and effect of these on the individuals associated within such institutions, are matters subject to factual observation, classification, and prediction. Indeed, this kind of factual information constitutes a rapidly developing body of knowledge, contributed to by all factual inquiries, from an examination of the effects of diet or the psychological problems of old age to an analysis of the disposition of the "organization man." To be sure, some such inquiries tend to be methodologically inexact, unable to resist the temptation of overhasty generalization. Yet, this kind of data, when reliable, provides the only explanation of disposition and of the disposition to obedience on which the authority of law and the legal state must finally rest. The problem of analysis here is complicated; the baffling complexity of a constantly shifting kaleidoscope of fact makes any generalization difficult and all prediction sorely limited.

However limited or hazardous, calculation of disposition on the basis of factual analysis of the institutional structure in all its complexity is an essential preliminary of legal speculation and construction. It is amazing and alarming that we continually try to oversimplify this arduous task by the substitution of dubious moral pronouncements for analysis. All good and right-thinking men ought to accept our law, we are likely to claim, either overtly or by implication, because our law is "right" or "just" or "Christian." What we are actually saying is that all men ought to manifest a disposition to obedience similar to that produced by our institutional structure. The

implication that the individual who has not had the good for-
tune to enjoy our social and institutional structure, and hence
no opportunity to acquire a disposition similar to our own, is
thereby immoral or insincere or obtusely stupid is surely a
most remarkable piece of impertinence.[4]

The intent of the present discussion does not extend to an
elaboration of the particular and specific facts of institutional
structure; from the specialized analysis of these facts we can
derive—if we will attend to them—useful hypotheses and pre-
dictions in regard to the profoundly important disposition to
obedience. Our present task, a more speculative one, proceeds
on the acceptance of this factual basis of the authority of law.
At this point we might indeed stop; we might contend that,
with the establishment of the factual basis of the authority of
law, our philosophy of law is complete and adequate. In traditional terms our evidence would be "historical," and systematic differences historically relative. The authority of law is
what it is because the disposition to obedience is what it is
because the institutional structure is what it is.

It appears, then, that when we examine the *factual* basis of
the authority of law, we must concede the irrelevance of other
claims to establish or support that authority. However, this
point is only half of the significant conclusion forced upon us
by the analysis of political authority. The observation that
moral judgment cannot provide a factual ground for political
authority implies nothing else whatever about the nature of
moral judgment. Political authority, however factual, does not
entail moral acceptability. At this point we must insist upon
some reasonable clarity and consistency of linguistic reference,
and require that certain distinctions which ought to be rather
evident be maintained in our discourse. The description of the
factual basis of legal authority does not establish anything

4. It should not surprise us, therefore, that a foreign policy and an approach
to "international law" based precisely and sometimes offensively on just such
premises are resented by other institutional configurations (states). The resentment which is a normal reaction does not facilitate communication and agreement.

whatever about the *desirability* of that authority or its practical results. This distinction of factual analysis and value judgment seems so elementary that the stubborn persistence of otherwise reasonable men in identifying or confusing these two essentially different activities is almost incomprehensible. The assumption that the desirability of law will establish its authority, or that to establish the authority of law makes it desirable, is a compound of confusion.[5] I contend that while the factual authority of a law might have to be acknowledged, I am not thereby obligated to proclaim that law acceptable or good. A sharp distinction is implied between factual analysis and moral discrimination; this distinction is a sensible, indeed mandatory, requirement of rational discourse. There is here a definitive assumption that should be explicated: namely, that law is the application of intelligence to the control and direction of individual and institutional relationships within a political structure. Such a definition suggests, of course, that individual and institutional relations *are* subject to modification and control by intelligence for some discriminated purpose. In all of the descriptions of the institutional structure as historically determined—whether the determinism be metaphysical, economic, or merely materialistically sequential, the question of law as intelligent control would be reduced to a surd, and legal and political theory confined to factual analysis.

The Marxist-Soviet development of legal theory and practice is a case in point. The original "orthodox" Marxist theory of law as exerting authority derived solely from the bourgeois economic structure made the claim of factual validity. With the destruction of that economic institution, the source and ground of the authority of law would be removed, and hence both the necessity and the authority of law would disappear in the new economically classless society. There was some degree of validity in this factual claim, but the degree was very

5. In this initial statement of the general distinction, indulgence is asked for the use of "desirability" in the terms of ordinary discourse. What specific sense can be given to this term will be the subject of later discussions, especially in chap. vi.

slight because of the unrealistic restriction of Marxist analysis to only one facet of the complex institutional structure of society. The fundamental error of the Marxist theory of law was myopic oversimplification. However, with the establishment of the Soviet state, this description of law very quickly proved *undesirable,* and Pashukanis and his "market-place" legal theory were liquidated (1937). The new theory of law was designed to accomplish what was *desired* by those holding a monopoly of power, and the revision began as soon as there was any real anticipation of actually acquiring that power (e.g., in Lenin, *State and Revolution*). The fact that this "desirability" did not of itself give authority to the law led immediately to the substitution of sheer force for legal authority. The prediction of the limits of force as a substitute for authority is very tenuous; there seem to be limits, however unassignable, to wholesale slaughter. At any rate, the Soviet leaders discovered that in certain areas, notably agriculture, the established disposition could be so negative as to be a disposition to *disobedience,* and that in such instances the continued application of force could be *institutionally* self-defeating, however ruthless in respect to the destruction of individuals. Individuals may be expendable, but institutions are not. The establishment of wage and prestige differentials, a complete deviation from the "classless ideology," represents an effort to establish *legal authority.* It would be a costly mistake to underestimate the extent to which, and the manner in which, this has been accomplished. True, what has resulted is not a theory of law consistent with Marxist ideology. The "communist society" has become the "socialist economy"; the "dictatorship of the proletariat" has become the "machinery of party power"; the "administration of things" has become the "discipline of citizens"; the state which was to wither away has become a nationalistic imperialist power.[6]

6. See C. B. Hoover, *The Economy, Liberty, and the State* (New York, 1959) and "The Soviet State Fails to Wither," *Foreign Affairs,* Vol. XXXI, No. 1 (1952), pp. 114-127.
    One of the best sources for the documents which formalize these philosophi-

Present Soviet legal theory is closer to the Hegelian than to the old Marxist ideology; the claim for the authority of law is grounded in the institutional structure of the state, including the "socialist" economy together with the political and other institutional areas. While the claim is made that this theory of law and the state is scientific or realistic, Soviet theorists betray the old confusion of fact and value in their claim for the "historical" validity of their institutional pattern, and hence the ultimate validity of their legal authority. This is the political philosophy of Hegel, and the refusal to call the identification of fact and value a "metaphysical" assumption does not at all change the nature of the legal theory that results from it.

Actually, the development of a Soviet philosophy for which it is most difficult to find derivation or support in Marxist philosophy indicates much more than mere theoretical deviation or "enrichment."[7] Russian political philosophy—and perhaps many aspects of Russian behavior—can be better understood if seen as the molding of ideological theories into channels and patterns of institutional development long established. Contemporary Soviet thought, in many respects, bears more resemblance to the Pan-Slavic philosophy of the nineteenth century than to "international" Marxism. Nikolai IA. Danilevskii (1822-1885) was a representative and influential spokesman

---

cal and legal changes in Soviet doctrine is *Soviet Legal Philosophy,* ed. John N. Hazard, trans. H. B. Babb (Cambridge, 1951).

Quite recently there has become available what is surely the most extensive and definitive statement of Soviet philosophy yet available, in *Fundamentals of Marxism-Leninism* (Foreign Languages Publishing House, Moscow, 1961; obtainable from Four Continent Book Corporation, New York). Some 250 pages of this 900 page work are devoted to an exposition of the latest version of Marxist-Leninist-Soviet philosophy.

7. A rather enlightening illustration of the difference between "enrichment" and "deviation" is provided in the reply by two Moscow philosophers (in *Voprosy filosofii*) to an article by a Polish philosopher, "The Permanent vs. the Transistory Interpretation of Marxism" (in *Nowa kultura*). After a bitter attack on the Pole as a deviationist, the Moscow philosophers show how Lenin enriched Marxist philosophy; oddly enough, Lenin's enrichment and the Pole's deviation turn out to be quite similar. See *The Current Digest of the Soviet Press,* Vol. IX, No. 38 (Oct. 30, 1957), pp. 3-6.

This Polish philosopher, Leszek Kolakowsky, has recently been again in the news because of a quite satirical play, which unaccountably managed to run for four days in Warsaw. See *The New York Times Magazine,* Feb. 18, 1962.

for Pan-Slavism, presenting a philosophy of history which is extraordinarily pertinent to the analysis of present Soviet political thought.[8]

Danilevskii rejected Hegel's monistic description of the historical process; in rather startling anticipation of Spengler,[9] and of some aspects of Toynbee, he describes cultures or civilizations as relatively independent, manifesting characteristics analogous to the biological organism which is born, flowers, decays, and dies. Yet, throughout his argument runs the same strong assumption of historic inevitability that marks the Hegelian and Marxist interpretations of history.

According to Danilevskii there are four essential ingredients in a fully developed civilization or culture: the religious, the political, the technological and artistic, and the socio-economic. The Hebrew, Greek, and Roman worlds were single-ingredient cultures, developing respectively the religious, the artistic, and the political. Western Europe has developed two cultural qualities: the political and the technological-artistic. The Pan-Slavic Federation, says Danilevskii, will develop all four of these essentials of mature civilization, and it will be especially strong in the socio-economic. With this development a new era of world history will begin. The predicted composition of the Pan-Slavic Federation is most interesting: Danilevskii included every "satellite" country. He also included Greece, and recent history records that only the valiant defense of a people for whom the institution of freedom is older than the institutions of Russia forestalled the realization of that prediction. It is also significant that he included Hun-

8. *Rossiya i Europa*. This work first appeared in the journal *Zarya* in 1869. The first book edition was dated 1871, but the edition of 1888 was the most widely read. A German translation was published in 1920: *Russland und Europa; eine Untersuchung über die kulturellen und politischen Beziehungen der slawischen zur germanisch-romanischen Welt*; übersetzt und eingeleitet von Karl Nötzel (Stuttgart, 1920). See also K. P. Pobyedonostseff, *Reflections of a Russian Statesman*, trans. R. C. Long (London, 1898). An interesting commentary is provided by N. S. Timasheff, "Russia and Europe," in *Thought*, Vol. XXIII, No. 8 (1948), pp. 21-35.

9. See the comment on Danilevskii in H. E. Barnes and H. Becker, *Social Thought from Lore to Science* (New York, 1938), II, 1032-1033: "His theories . . . have been revived in recent years by the German writer Oswald Spengler, who, however, steadfastly avoids any mention of his debt to his Russian predecessor. The parallelism is too close to be accidental."

gary but not Austria. Of Poland, object of particularly con-
ciliatory treatment by the U.S.S.R., Danilevskii remarks that
its future is uncertain, but that Poland would be well-advised
to join the Pan-Slavic Federation. Is it not to Danilevskii and
to Pobyedonostseff that we should look for understanding of
the present philosophy of the U.S.S.R., rather than to the
worn shibboleths of Marxism?

The Anglo-American development of political philosophy
has also perpetuated a confusion of fact and value, of authority and justification; but the nature of the confusion is
somewhat difficult from the tour de force identification characteristic of the Hegelian and Marxist political theories. Ours
has been a method of reduction, an attempt to accomplish by
definition the elimination of any discrepancy or distinction
between fact and value. Characteristically, this attempt has
taken the form of denying validity to anything that is not factually verifiable—verifiable, that is, in the extraordinarily limited definitive terms acceptable to this kind of theorist. So
enamored does he become with the process of reduction that
he seems prepared to disregard a substantial part of his data
in order to accomplish it.

It would be unfair to place the blame for this curious and
continued fault on any one person, but certainly John Stuart
Mill did give the procedure a statement which is classic in its
simplicity. When Mill proceeded from the assertion that "the
only proof capable of being given that an object is visible is
that people actually see it" to the argument that "the sole
evidence it is possible to produce that anything is desirable is
that people do actually desire it," he provided so simple a formulation of the reduction of value to fact that simple-minded
people continue to this day to use the same argument. Mill
was indeed guilty of semantic oversimplification, but to assume
that he implied the absurdities of reduction indulged in by
later ethicists is most unjust.[10]

The interesting fact about Mill's argument—and all such

10. For a comment on the general misinterpretation of Mill's argument, see
James Ward Smith, *op. cit.,* pp. 71 ff.

reductive procedures, from the standpoint of our consideration of law, authority, desirability, and moral judgment—is
the remarkable ease with which this kind of argument simply
ignores an essential ingredient of the action situation with
which it is purportedly concerned. It is true that men see what
they see, but it is equally true and just as important that men
can see more than they do see. Men did, in fact, want to see
more, and they invented spectacles, telescopes, and micro-
scopes. As a result of this activity—not at all a consequence of
the facts themselves—the facts of science, of human action, of
law and morals were transformed. It just will not do to leave
out of our analysis of action the factor of value judgment.

Men make judgments that they do not like facts as they find
them, and they also make judgments that they would like to
have values which present facts do not make possible. Something almost aggressively obtuse and antirational is evidenced
in statements such as that by Weldon: "There is no sense in
asking what ought to happen, or what would happen under
imaginary ideal conditions, and disputes on such points are
purely verbal and a waste of time."[11] Consider the same kind
of confusion in language evidenced by Glanville Williams:

> What is important is a subjective matter. Importance lies
> in the eye of the beholder. No operation can be performed
> to test whether one feature of a referent is more important
> than the others, nor is such an operation conceivable. To
> debate what is important and what unimportant is, there-
> fore, to enter upon a controversy that can only be settled
> by the emotional conversion of one of the parties.[12]

In a sense, the function of judgment, and most certainly of
judicial judgment, is precisely the determination of what is
"important," and it is a contortion of meaning to describe this
action as mere "emotional conversion." It is not descriptive
language that is being used in such statements, but non-de-

11. *Op. cit.*, p. 13.
12. "The Controversy Concerning the Word 'Law,'" in *Philosophy, Politics and Society*, ed. P. Laslett (New York, 1956), p. 142.

scriptive, assumptive language, and the nature of the assumption deprives it of any form of justification.[13]

Men can and do make judgments which are justified on grounds more substantial than feeling or emotion of disposition. It would seem that any sensible discussion or moral judgment must start from some such premises as those asserted, for instance, by C. I. Lewis:

> The primary and pervasive significance of knowledge lies in its guidance of action: knowing is for the sake of doing. And action, obviously, is rooted in evaluation. For a being which did not assign comparative values, deliberate action would be pointless; and for one which did not know, it would be impossible. . . .
>
> The interest of action is not an interest in what is before us, on its own account, but an interest in what will be or may be. And the interest of that knowledge of the world which guides our action is the same.[14]

There is something refreshing in the plain, uncomplicated language of John Dewey when he discusses this problem of moral judgment:

> Then it surprisingly turns out that the primary significance of the unique and morally ultimate character of the concrete situation is to transfer the weight and burden of morality to intelligence. It does not destroy responsibility; it only locates it. A moral situation is one in which judgment and choice are required antecedently to overt action. The practical meaning of the situation— that is to say the action needed to satisfy it—is not self-evident. It has to be searched for. There are conflicting desires and alternative apparent goods. What is needed is to find the right course of action, the right good.[15]

13. Compare, for example, a reasonable statement of the context of judgment by John Rawls, "Justice as Fairness," in *Justice and Social Policy,* ed. F. A. Olafson (New York, 1961), p. 107: "I have tried to set out the kind of principles upon which judgments concerning the justice of practices may be said to stand. The analysis will be successful to the degree that it expresses the principles involved in these judgments when made by competent persons upon deliberation and reflection. . . . Societies will differ from one another not in having or failing to have this notion [the concept of justice] but in the range of cases in which they apply it and in the emphasis which they give it as compared with other moral concepts."

14. *An Analysis of Knowledge and Evaluation* (La Salle, Illinois, 1946), p. 2.

15. *Reconstruction in Philosophy* (New York, 1920), pp. 163-164.

The recognition that men do act in this way does not mean that facts are ignored or distorted; it means that rational action cannot be defined merely in terms of factual assertion, and it may, and in many instances does, mean that factual assertions will be subject to modification by moral judgment.[16] Surely a sensible observation of the circumstances of action requires us to distinguish the following kinds of statements, and to admit that they reflect observable situations of action in society:

"I will obey this law because I think it is right."
"I don't agree with this law, but I'll obey it."
"I don't agree with this law, and I'll obey it only under protest."
"I don't think this law is right, and I won't obey it unless I'm forced to."
"This law is wrong, and I won't obey it under any circumstances."

Neither democrat nor dictator can afford to ignore the implications of this range of individual judgment, and yet it is at precisely this crucial point in the analysis of action that we seem most muddled. Neither identification nor reduction will alter the historical fact that such judgments are made and acted upon, whether it be in democratic demonstrations or in the streets of Budapest, and it takes a remarkable kind of obtuseness to deny that they affect and alter subsequent factual situations. Any situation which brings into question the authority of law, as we have described it here, must mean one of two things: either the promulgated law is contrary to the disposition to obedience on the part of those to whom it is addressed, or for some reason the individual finds himself in disagreement with his own disposition which would have in-

16. It is difficult to understand why those one would suppose to be vitally interested in the function of judgment—moralists, philosophers, political theorists—cling so tenaciously to a methodology which no reputable physical scientist, supposedly concerned exclusively with facts, would today try to support. For example, see Victor Lenzen, *Causality in Natural Science* (Springfield, Illinois, 1954); Philipp Frank, *Philosophy of Science* (New York, 1957).

clined him to accept the law. Either situation presents the law with a critical problem, but the first case is easier of analysis than the second. Law which is so contrary to the prevailing disposition to obedience that it is legally unenforceable must be repealed or altered—as in the case of Soviet agricultural laws or the Eighteenth Amendment in the United States; the alternative is enforcement by non-legal methods.[17] The institutional structure of society and its influence upon the individual are facts which can be observed and analyzed, however mistaken these procedures may be in particular instances.

In respect to judgment, however, we seem even less clear as to its nature and effectiveness than we are about the relation of disposition to authority, and that is very unclear indeed. The terms of ordinary discourse used in the five statements above—"right," "agree," "protest"—convey the indefiniteness of our understanding of what is here in relation and in conflict. The action of the individual in response to the asserted authority of law may be a very complicated confusion of factual disposition and evaluative judgment. (We must say "may be" because the five statements do not comprehend the situation in which the individual does not reflect or make a judgment; in such cases, no evaluation of the law or question of its authority is involved.) Not much sense can be made then of any appraisal of the authority of law unless we have some reasonable clarity about what operates to induce individuals to accept and obey, reject but obey, or reject and defy, the law. At the risk of being offensively elementary or tiresomely repetitive, it must be insisted that we try to distinguish, and to recognize the distinction, between disposition as fact and judgment as evaluation.

At the outset, let us discriminate contrary-to-fact assumptions in respect to the institutional structure of society and the individuals within that structure. There is a field of speculation where institutions are hypothetically constructed to sup-

17. By "non-legal" is meant the application of force beyond the defined limits of legal and judicial procedures.

port a previsioned system of values. This area of indulgent manipulation comprehends the almost limitless ranges of utopian construction. Utopian literature occupies a peculiar and privileged position in the large expanse of man's evaluative constructions. The utopist is fancy-free; his medium is fiction, even though his intent may be very real. Hence, his selected form of expression allows him to ignore fact, to construct or to imagine any condition of factual circumstance which will serve the purpose of his exposition. His time may be past, present, or five thousand years in the future; his spatial location may be here, there, or nowhere. His state is at once the *outopia* of no place and the *eutopia* of the good place. Utopia is the ideal society unencumbered by dissonant fact. This latitude of imagination makes utopian literature one of the most fertile sources of information about the historical development of man's moral and political ideals, and more attention to the progressive continuity of utopian construction would have contributed to our understanding of present ideals and values.

Interesting and valuable as we may consider utopian thought, however, it is clearly distinguishable from political philosophy; the task of this discipline is considerably more difficult, even if not more profound. Certainly, political philosophy is not concerned merely with measurement, comparison, and manipulation, wholly uninterested in the values with which the utopist is concerned. That which purports to be philosophical analysis is committed to a concern for values, their speculative definition, their meaning, and their effective realization. In its specification as *political* philosophy, this analysis must evidence an initial and continuing acknowledgment and description of the pertinent facts of the political process, for the concern here is not only with the consideration of values, but with their realization, and it is with *facts* that political values must be realized. Ambiguity in regard to fact will mean disillusionment in respect to values.

Recognition of the two essential ingredients of political

thought indicates the most serious difficulty of that enterprise. The distinction of factual statements and value judgments is a persistent and perplexing problem in political thought. The necessity to discriminate clearly between fact and value is not peculiar to political philosophy and political theory, but it is perhaps more ubiquitous and difficult in this area than in the other social sciences, and certainly not amenable to the rather sharp differentiation that is possible in most of the procedures of the so-called physical sciences. Such discrimination is a task which requires the sharpest and most constant vigilance on the part of the political theorist, for the failure to recognize and maintain the distinction of fact and value leads inevitably to a confused muddle of morals and law, of means and ends, of policy-making and administrative procedures.

Resolution of the duality of fact and value by the specious process of reducing one to the other has been an almost commonplace method in the history of thought, but repetitive effort has not made more sensible or palatable the technique which achieves consistency by an intellectual purging of the inconsistent. The positivism which eliminates values by proclaiming facts alone to be "real," and the determinism which distorts fact by dogmatic assignment of metaphysical or religious value, are both guilty, either of fraud or of the most elementary kind of mistake in analysis. It ought not to require a tortuous philosophical argument to support the claim that political speculation which proceeds in ignorance of fact, or with erroneous definitions of fact, will prove considerably less than realistic or fruitful. On the other hand, political analysis which confines itself to the mere description and assertion of "facts" may provide interesting statistical tabulation, but little else.

There is no special kind of thinking that is appropriate to the facts of politics and political philosophy. Correct thinking is correct thinking, and in any field it begins with the definition and description of subject matter. True, in different areas we attend to different aspects of a subject, and we devise instruments of observation which are useful to this deliberately limited kind of observation. There is, however, no particular subject matter which is the exclusive property of a specific kind of observation; trees are just as appropriate a subject of investigation for economics and politics as for botany or forestry. At the moment the political implications of water are just as significant in Pakistan and India as are its chemical properties. Clearly, the more limited our observation is, the more precise it is likely to be. More exactitude and precision can be expected from the analysis of the chemical composition of Pakistan's present water supply than could be anticipated from a meteorological prediction of the future quantity of that supply. The scientific analysis of the water provides an essential part of the factual ground on which assessment of use and control can be properly based; thus do the facts of all the sciences furnish the material on which fruitful political speculation and judgment can proceed. To ignore these facts in mere assertion or propagandizing of a particular value judgment is the same as to ask one ignorant of the pertinent facts to arbitrate the allocation of the available supply of water. Ignorance of fact may be characteristic of the amateur; distortion of fact is the mark of the charlatan.

To be sure, the description of political fact is difficult; happy-thought construction may be for some an escape, but it is not a substitute for the hard task of factual discrimination. It might be argued that the data of political philosophy are more comprehensive than those of any other discipline, and even that its data are sometimes remarkably inaccessible to observation. Political philosophy cannot expect to achieve the precision of judgment possible in descriptive enterprises which can minutely limit and freely manipulate their data; but this is not an excuse for political philosophy to abandon factual analysis in an indulgence of fantasy.[18]

18. "The representation of natural objects in precise classifications and the maintenance of Agreement in regard to objects of use—the coordination of these two functions is what we ordinarily mean by *control*. Control is, in general, the area in which an emphasis is made upon the attainment of order or Law in the

I have called judgments *based* on fact "value" judgments, and so they are. The water engineer is an expert; his expertness consists in his knowledge of facts—analytic and predictive —*and* his ability to utilize this complex aggregation of facts to arrive at a reasonable judgment. Consider, now, how much more complex and profound is the task of the engineer if we ask him to tell us whether the distribution of the water supply is legal or just or good, or even whether it is a "fair" resolution of the problem. Yet it is precisely this kind of judgment which is the ultimate—and often the immediate and critical—concern of political philosophy, or rather a series of such judgments comprehending an inexhaustible range of factual data. In such a grandiose undertaking, it is less than sensible to proceed without great care and considerable modesty. Disaster is the inevitable result when the witless or the dabblers or the dogmatists make political judgments. The minimum of care that we must evidence is a proper concern for the facts of political structure. Without such concern, our value judgments will be empty symbols more conducive to confusion than clarity.

No argument is necessary to support the contention that ambiguity in value discrimination cannot fail to produce confusion in action, and the almost certain futility of disillusionment. Men who are unclear about what they mean by "liberty" and "equality" are the more readily persuaded by promises of "security" and "superiority." Our present confusion about the nature and function of values in the political process and structure is not the result of moral apathy or, as is often suggested, the prevalence of a materialistic philosophy; nor is the confusion to be relieved by dogmatic assertion of faith, be it secular or sectarian. The problem has resulted directly from a plain

State, when State is the organization of institutions. Another term, which is more specific, is *Administration.* . . .Thus, we do not expect the administrator to act with the remarkable precision of the physical scientist, nor yet maintain the degree of agreement brought about by the vocational scientist; but we must demand that his activity be directed toward the maintenance of order in relation to material institutions. This order will take the form of Law" (Glenn Negley, *The Organization of Knowledge* [New York, 1942], pp. 159, 161; see also Albert Lepawsky, *Administration: The Art and Science of Organization and Management* [New York, 1949], pp. 664-667).

inadequacy of observation and description. We are unclear about values because we have not understood the nature of values, and we do not comprehend the essential nature of value because we have not properly distinguished political fact from moral value.

At this level of elementary description and definition, our own political philosophy of the past hundred years or so presents a rather dismal picture. We seem considerably less clear about the values integral and essential to a democratic political structure than were democratic philosophers and spokesmen of the eighteenth and nineteenth centuries. Mill's essay *On Liberty* is a ringing historical classic of our tradition, and while it must be admitted that the clarion quality of that ringing was partly achieved by distributive emphasis, Mill was more astute about fundamental value conflicts in the representative process than some of his overeager critics seem aware. It is very odd that American political philosophy, apparently so much under the influence of the empirical and the pragmatic, should have been so profoundly neglectful of the factual in the political structure. To a large extent, it has been the ignorance of fact that has produced the confusion in value discrimination. Our political attention has been almost belligerently disdainful of regard for the fundamental facts of social structure—institutions. This disregard has been reflected in the casual lack of concern for that branch of government whose function it is to achieve order in that institutional configuration: administration. As late as 1928 John Dickinson could remark correctly:

> The term "Administrative Law" has been knocking at the ears of common lawyers with increasing insistence the last twenty years, but they have as yet responded with no eagerly receptive hospitality. . . . But whether or not we will admit any traffic with the term "Administrative Law," we must recognize that there has been growing up in spite of us in the statutes and decisions of the last few decades a body of law for which there is as yet no rubric in the books.[19]

19. *American Bar Association Journal*, Vol. XIV, No. 9 (1928), 513.

The expression "in spite of us" augurs poorly for political and legal philosophy.

The legislative-executive-judicial model became so fixed in our political theory and language that the terms *administration* and *administrator* had only the vaguest assignable meanings, and hence were infrequently used; "the administration" meant in an indefinite kind of way the regime of a particular political party. In our laudable effort to establish a system of representative legislation, one of the most significant elements of our Greek and Roman political heritage, their attention to administration, was all but lost to sight. It is, for instance, unfortunate for us and for Plato that his political philosophy is usually presented to students in the established, but very ambiguous, model of a "guardian-ruler" monopoly of power. Even the slightest attention to the language of the *Laws* shows how carefully Plato tried to distinguish the functions of lawgiver (νομοθέτη s) and guardian of the law (νομοφύλαξ); the distinction occurs in Book I and continues throughout the work. There is, to be sure, some ambiguity in the description of these functions, but there is no doubt that the guardians of the law are to be mainly concerned with administration. "Guarding" the law means seeing to it that the purpose of the law is in practice achieved; their duties range from policing the markets to consultation with the director of education. Recognition of the importance assigned by Plato to trained and responsible administrators is a noteworthy correction to the usual and sometimes distorted explication of his political and legal philosophy. One need not subscribe to his philosophy to acknowledge and appreciate his emphasis on administrative responsibility—and to regret that this aspect of his *Laws* has been almost wholly neglected.[20]

To be sure, in the past thirty years there has been a flurry of attention to problems of professional administrative activity, personnel, decision-making, civil service organization, and

20. See the exhaustive and definitive work of Glenn R. Morrow, *Plato's Cretan City: A Historical Interpretation of the* Laws (Princeton, 1960).

the like. Yet we are substantially unclear and undecided on matters concerning the relation of this political administration of the vast area of fact in the political structure to the essentially evaluative functions of legislation and adjudication.[21] It is a rather startling paradox that Marxism, anti-idealist and strenuously "scientific," and democracy, claiming proudly the heritage of British empiricism, should both indulge in disregard for fact to the extent of assuming that the administration of institutional fact in the political structure would be autonomous or self-administering if only the political power were oriented to the proper values. It is unfortunate that more attention has not been paid to Mill's scrupulous empirical method which admitted facts he found undeniable, even though they presented problems of accommodation. He saw the inevitable difficulties of trying to combine in a single office the functions of representative president and executive administrator.

> A most important principle of good government in a popular constitution is that no executive functionaries should be appointed by popular election: neither by the votes of the people themselves, nor by those of their representatives. The entire business of government is skilled employment; the qualifications for the discharge of it are of that special and professional kind which cannot be properly judged of except by persons who have themselves some share of those qualifications, or some practical experience of them. . . . When the highest dignity in the State is to be conferred by popular election once in

21. A lucid and succinct statement of the opposing philosophies of three theories of administration is "Emerging Conflicts in the Doctrines of Public Administration," by Herbert Kaufman, *The American Political Science Review*, L (1956), 1057-1073. E.g., ". . . an examination of the administrative institutions of this country suggests that they have been organized and operated in pursuit successively of three values, here designated representativeness, neutral competence, and executive leadership. . . . The tendencies toward division reinforce each other and there are no visible factors thrusting toward alliances like that fortuitous one developed by a peculiar conjunction of circumstances during the infancy of public administration as an academic and occupational speciality. As a result, the language of public administration is likely to become increasingly strategic and tactical in tone rather than 'scientific.' . . . The question that will be asked about suggested reorganizations is not 'What, according to the canons of management science, is the best organization?' but, 'What will be the effect of this measure on the institution we support?'"

every few years, the whole intervening time is spent in what is virtually a canvass. President, ministers, chiefs of parties, and their followers, are all electioneerers; the whole community is kept intent on the mere personalities of politics, and every public question is discussed and decided with less reference to its merits than to its expected bearing on the presidential election.[22]

The description and relation of executive representative leadership and executive administrative control are certainly not easy in theory, much less in practice; the problem will not be made easier by inattention to fact. Our lack of concern for administration as a specialized function of government was the direct result of a failure to observe and define the nature of the institutions which are the factual structure of any political society. Institutions are the most elementary of political facts; they are, indeed, more elementary than individuals, since for any given polity at any given time the institutions existed before the individuals. There is no evaluative significance in this statement; it is merely an assignment of factual status. There is a vast amount of sociological analysis of this kind of factual data; our attention can be more profitably directed to a consideration of the way in which our legal and political theory treats this institutional area of fact in contemporary thinking.

As objects of political or legal attention, institutions are more properly termed corporate entities, or simply corporations. Consider the manner in which we have described and defined such an essential ingredient of our political structure as the corporation. It is a matter of rather elementary observation that corporate entities are facts; a university or General Motors or the Roman Catholic Church is not an ideal or a myth or a fiction. We are surrounded and enmeshed by corporate organizations; while they are indeed complex, they are neither hidden nor mysterious. Why then has our political and legal philosophy insisted upon treating these facts as "fictions," as, for example, in the persistent definition of these observable,

22. *Considerations on Representative Government* (London, 1861), chap. xiv.

factual corporate structures as "persons"? To define a university as a person makes little sense, if any sense at all, and it only compounds the nonsense when the definition is made even more meaningless by saying that such a corporate body is a "fictitious" person. Such is the description of fact that we are offered by our philosophy of law and politics, an instance of primitive description which approaches the anthropomorphism of ignorance. To call an institution a "person" is quite the same as if I were to call student John Smith a "university"; yet, because I know very well that John Smith is not a university, I call him a "fictitious" university. This kind of game might be fun in a nursery school, but it is a sorry substitute for thinking about facts which require legislation and administration. Observe this playroom of jargon built for politics and law by our philosophy; while those who are entrusted with the only means for maintaining order in society, namely, law, romp merrily and noisily in this world of make-believe, the hard, real facts of institutional development overcome reason by expediency, replace value by accident. To be sure, it is not now customary to use the term "person" in referring to a corporate organization, but the juristic theory of corporate personality imposed a definitive framework which persists to distort meaning.[23] In fact, increasing diffidence about the use of

23. I realize that many who are sophisticated in legal and political theory will very likely remark that *nobody* uses such language any more. While citation of an encyclopedia might for some purposes be questionable, it certainly serves the purpose of reflecting current and literate expression and usage. The 1962 edition of *Collier's Encyclopedia*, under the heading "Corporation Law," gives the following definition: "A corporation is an association of persons treated by the law as a unit, with rights and duties and a life separate and apart from those of its members. Formed according to a prescribed ritual, this 'person' or separable entity, as it is called, has attributes recognized by law. . . . A corporation is, moreover, recognized under the U. S. Constitution as a 'person,' entitled to 'due process' under the Fifth and Fourteenth amendments and under the 'equal protection' clause of the latter amendment. By contrast it is not a 'citizen'. . . ."
The 1963 edition of the *Encyclopedia Britannica*, under the heading "Corporation," asserts: "A corporation is a fictitious legal person. . . ."
Cf.: "The statement that the corporation is a legal entity means that it has the rights of a person so far as the law is concerned and that the courts recognize it as a person. . . . The principal characteristics of the corporation result from the fiction that it is a legal person. . . . The theory that the corporation is a separate, legal artificial person may be said to be definitely established as a part of the law" (Richard N. Owens, *Business Organization and Combination* [Englewood Cliffs, N. J., 1961], pp. 108, 109, 123).

the word "person" is simply an indication that the lack of sense became evident even in legal discourse.[24]

Uncritical and abortive comments on the subject of "fictions" are plentiful in our literature, with very little attention to the real nature of the fictional device. A strong case can be made for the use of "as if" postulates in metaphysical speculation (as employed by Kant, for example in the *Critique of Practical Reason*). In legal and political thought, the fiction has historically been used to obscure intent, to conceal ignorance of fact, or to present value judgments under the pretense of factual statements.[25] The employment of a reasonable fiction to supplement knowledge in a speculative endeavor which transcends all available fact is one thing; to use the device of fiction as a substitute for the proper description of available and observable fact is quite another matter. Make-believe is an aceptable device in utopian construction; in political and legal theory it is a crude fallacy. The persistence of the fallacy, either overtly or implicitly, has made impossible any sensible definition of the important concept of *responsibility;* by admitting only "personal" responsibility we fail any method of describing or assessing corporate responsibility.

Our Anglo-American tradition has been eminently successful in describing and defining the *individual,* a necessary part of the task of political philosophy. There is no reason whatever to bemoan what individualism has accomplished; it has been a noteworthy and valuable contribution to our understanding of one of the factual ingredients of political organiza-

24. There may be substantial reasons, historical and expedient, for the employment of the "corporate personality" fiction in legal procedure. The corporate entity had to be brought within the purview of the law somehow or other. Procedural expediency, however, is not a substitute for analysis and description; the analogical nonsense indulged in by so-called "organic" political theory cannot be excused by reference to legal expediency.

For an effort to describe sensibly one kind of corporate structure, the economic, see Adolph A. Berle, Jr. and Gardiner C. Means, *The Modern Corporation and Private Property* (New York, 1932), and other writings of Berle on this subject.

25. Interesting comment on the history of the juristic use of fiction is given by M. Georges Cornil, "Réflexions sur le Rôle de la Fiction dans le Droit," *Archives de Philosophie du droit et de Sociologie juridique*, Nos. 3-4, 1935, pp. 28-42; and also the work which occasioned Cornil's remarks: René Dekkers, *La fiction juridique* (Paris, 1935).

tion. It is regrettable that we did not proceed to a similar description of the remaining and equally obvious area of fact that we have here designated only vaguely as the "institutional." There seems little excuse for this single-minded myopia, for institutions are an integral, undeniable, and manifest fact of any society. Too, institutions have received rather profound descriptive attention in traditions of political thought other than our own, and some attention to this corporate philosophy would have been instructive.

The apparent reason for our adoption of the improper term "person" as descriptive of institution was the fact that the definitive framework of our political philosophy is exclusively individualistic. When we subject an area of fact which is not individual to definition in terms which are suitable only to the description of individuals, we are perpetrating a kind of analogical transference which distorts the fact and produces meaningless judgments. In the same manner, corporate philosophy has rather characteristically insisted upon defining the individual solely in terms of the institution, and the result has been some very erroneous propositions about the nature of the individual in political society. Neither individualism nor corporatism can arrive at a reasonable judgment if the terms of that judgment are limited to a philosophy deliberately exclusive of a body of fact which is pertinent to political judgment.

CHAPTER VI

MORAL JUDGMENT

*We find everywhere the state asserting itself as a power
which has, and, if need be, asserts the right to make use
of and expend the property and person of the individual
without regard to his wishes, and which, moreover, may
destroy his life in punishment, and put forth other powers
such as no theory of contract will explain except by the
most palpable fictions, while at the same time no ordinary person calls their morality in question. Both history
and practical politics refuse to verify the 'facts' of the
individualists. . . .*

*The child is not fallen from heaven . . . . he has in him
inherited habits, or what will of themselves appear as
such; but, in addition to this, he is not for one moment
left alone, but continually tampered with; and the habit-
uation which is applied from the outside is the more insidious that it answers to this inborn disposition.*[1]

THE restricted kind of definition which admits as real fact
only the subjective individual has not only failed to define the fact of institution but, as might be expected, produced
only a partial description of the individual. We have continued to describe the status and function of individuals solely
in terms of their subjective properties, whereas it is clear that
an individual is something more than a mere subjectivity. An
individual within any kind of social organization—and I shall
here assume that there is no other kind of individual, at least
in a politically meaningful sense—has a describable *objective*
content which is derived from that social structure. The *structure* of society is institutional, and the nature of institutional
structure must be an ingredient of our descriptive observation

1. F. H. Bradley, *Ethical Studies* (London, 1876), pp. 149-155.

if we are to understand the individual as a political fact. The objective, corporate structure of society is precisely what our individualistic philosophy has not understood and has never properly defined. This failure makes the task of political philosophy extremely difficult; the student must undertake a description of fact which should be, but is not, a matter of historical acquaintance.

Such description is not easy, and it is rendered more difficult by the persistence of an ambiguous terminology which, in its subjectivistic emphasis, conceals and distorts the nature of non-subjective fact. Much of the muddled description of individual and institution, and especially the confusion of political fact and moral value, must be attributed to the shallow and superficial kind of thinking that has characterized the trend of ethical theory in the recent past. Our ethical theory has made the elementary mistake of assigning value connotation to that which ought to be defined factually. Value assignment, if it is to be sensible, must follow factual description; ascription of value is not a substitute for definition of fact, and to attempt the discrimination of values before clarifying the pertinent facts is a reversal of logical sequence. Our dominant ethical theory is a celebration of such illogical procedure.

The Utilitarian moral view, which is our philosophic heritage, issued in an unresolved dilemma, although both Bentham and Mill made some pertinent, if tentative, suggestions for further development which were ignored by subsequent ethical speculation. For Utilitarian ethics, the fundamental moral datum is some kind of subjective psychological interest, whatever form such interest may take. The erroneous description of the moral person as a purely subjective, discrete, and arbitrary entity has been perpetuated in the dominant ethical theory of recent British and American philosophy, which, despite its usually disdainful disregard of the historic Utilitarian position, has in fact remained in slavish bondage to the framework of descriptive definition established by the individualists. The Utilitarian argument had at least the advantage of recognizing the problem: that the assertion of a subjective arbitrary as the basis of morality reduced moral speculation to mere number theory, a counting of unique and discrete arbitraries or interests. Subjective "states of mind" are assertable, but not communicable; the Utilitarians faced the problem of achieving some kind of communication and order in a situation described factually as one of moral anarchy.[2] Bentham's tour de force assumption of pre-established harmony between private interests and public good did not resolve the dilemma; on the contrary, it focused attention on the sharp difference between the factual demands of political expediency and the realization of individual values subjectively determined.

The entire burden of the subjectivist development of moral theory does not, however, rest on Utilitarianism. Under the influence of a religious doctrine which asserts the primacy of an act of faith, and is itself therefore an extreme form of the subjective preference view, even such a rationalistic ethic as that of Kant is reduced by emphasis to psychological will theory. So effectively has this interpretation been established that it is necessary to show by exegesis of his work that Kant held as necessary and inescapable the sequence from natural man to legal citizen to moral person. At the point of moral judgment, a person is already a complicated political and legal being. The interpretation of Kant having been what it was, many readers find it almost unbelievable that he began his great work on religion with the assertion that "for its own sake morality does not need religion at all," although he personally felt that "morality leads ineluctably to religion."[3]

The partial and inadequate factual description of the moral person assumed by Utilitarianism has been generally accepted with uncritical fervor by ethicists who have henceforth been trying vainly to make factual sense out of a contrary-to-fact definition. Claiming to be realists, naturalists, and empiricists,

2. Cf. Glenn Negley, "The Failure of Communication in Ethics," in *Symbols and Values* (New York, 1954), pp. 647-653.
3. *Religion within the Limits of Reason Alone*, pp. 3-5.

they have in fact proclaimed a moral person completely unrealistic, unnatural, and empirically non-existent.[4] Actually,
the majority of what today passes for ethical theory should
properly be designated exercises in dubious epistemology;
since the epistemologist is characteristically interested, not in
truth, but in theories of truth, ethical speculation is thus two
degrees removed from the consideration and description of
fact.[5] Political theory has had little choice but to accept the
bad factual descriptions and the muddled definitions of moral
judgment bequeathed it by philosophy.[6] The psychological

4. *Cf.* S. Strasser, *Das Gemüt* (Freiburg, 1956).
  5. This kind of thing was well described by Bertrand Russell: "To discuss
endlessly what silly people mean when they say silly things may be amusing
but can hardly be important" *(Portraits from Memory and Other Essays* [Lon-
don, 1956], pp. 156-157).
  6. The failure of value theory to produce a meaningful description of the
moral person has forced some more perceptive social scientists to attempt such
a definition: e.g., "The individual absorbs or derives most of his values and
his goals . . . from the cultural milieu of the community. In fact some con-
stellations of cultural elements may become so internalized in the individual
and so much a part of his personality that he becomes very much bound by
them and by the relevant moral rules; to the extent that this is the case, the
community's cultural pattern may be said to have been internalized in the
self" (Joseph J. Spengler, "Sociological Value Theory, Economic Analyses, and
Economic Policy," *The American Economic Review*, XLIII, [1953], 340-349).
The terms in any such broad definition need to be clarified and specified, but
there is here at least a meaningful reference to the objective factual content of the individual. If these facts can be described, then some sense can be
made of the hitherto incomprehensible notion of individual subjective preference—but it will be factual sense, not moral denotation.
  There is one outstanding exception in recent philosophy to the kind of
ethical theory which merits the strictures of our argument here; understand-
ably, this philosopher has been almost totally ignored by philosophers and
political theorists—but note the philosophical analysis of precisely the observation made by Spengler in the above quotation: "The essence of the moral
person considered as a moral agent is just this system of objective relations,
relations whose terms are parts of the structure of things, to which he gives
expression in his acts. The person therefore becomes identified and identical
with the institutions of life, which are the common body of the multitude of
persons regarded as active agents. Culture therefore is this system of persons
as they have made themselves corporate in their objects. . . . The moral world
is, then, the total world in which acts have meaning; and the essence of meaning in every act and in every moral judgment lies in their expressing some
relation between the natural world and the cultural world as that relation
formulates itself in a personalized situation. The standard of principle for every
specific act and every specific judgment is contained in the objective and external situation, and this objective situation also defines the personal attitude
out of which the energies of the act flow, and the objective situation is determined in any specific case as that upon or within which these energies issue"
(E. Jordan, *The Good Life* [Chicago, 1949], pp. 436, 257; see also *Theory of
Legislation* [Chicago, 1952] and *Forms of Individuality* [Indianapolis, 1927]).

preference theory of morals, in its various forms, presents for the attention of political theory an aggregation of discrete subjectivities whose value discriminations are immediate, arbitrary, and essentially nothing more than mere states of feeling or preference. Such a definition of the basic data of the political structure sorely limits the constructive and speculative possibilities of political theory. How can order be achieved out of this conglomerate hodge-podge of infinite arbitraries? One alternative, ever present, is of course an authoritarian resolution, which may take the form of declaring heretical all those who do not assert a particular psychological preference, or the equally authoritarian manipulation of preferences through mass media of communication. In either case, any claim of authority will resolve into an assertion of force. The antirational reduction of moral discrimination to psychological states of immediacy has falsely defined the problem of political order for the political theorist; the development of nonrational and irrational political theories is an inevitable result of the use of a concept of person which does not satisfy the requirements of rational definition.

When the subjectivist gets religion, he manifests a strong tendency to become an authoritarian, but authoritarianism is a completely inconsistent position for one who asserts the subjectivity of moral data. The subjectivist can achieve authority only by ceasing to be a moralist and becoming a self-appointed legislator, who strives by force or fraud to impose his subjective will upon other less forceful or fraudulent subjective wills. If moralists could be moral to the extent of recognizing this inhibition which subjectivism imposes upon itself, the result might be a kind of salutary hedonism, for it is certainly questionable whether moral anarchy is not preferable to the self-electing fanaticism of the subjective preference which confuses its feeling-intensity with a drive for power. However, like the proponents of salvation by grace—to whom they are closely akin—the subjectivists seem never content to let others enjoy a different preference.

The Pragmatist development from this misconception of moral preference and rational definition was inevitable; it served the useful purpose of exhibiting sharply and unmistakably the result of failure to maintain the distinction of factual description and value discrimination. The description of the processes of rational inquiry, of observation and definition of fact, as inextricably mixed and confused with moral (that is, psychological) preference, is, of course, to make rational inquiry itself subject to the immediate, the arbitrary, and the non-rational. Pragmatism simply asserted baldly what had been implicit in the entire subjectivist description; it is a paradox of Instrumentalism that its description of rational inquiry deprives reason of its legitimate instrumental function.

It is difficult to assess the ethicists who rely upon a sheer assertion of preference as the only ground of moral discrimination. One must try to discern what they might possibly be trying to say from the vague, generalized, and indiscriminate language they use. H. A. Prichard, for example, when he argued that reason must be eliminated as an ingredient in moral evaluation, was apparently saying that what is good and right in any situation of moral choice will be immediately and self-evidently clear.[7] Surely he could not have meant anything so simple as this, for an individual's preference among available alternatives, not rationally or evaluatively assessed, is a manifestation of the disposition which he has accumulated in the institutional configuration to which he has been exposed. What else he could have meant is not readily apparent, and if this is what he did indeed mean, then he is not talking about moral evaluation at all, but rather about the factual evidence of a disposition institutionally determined. Weldon seems almost eager to suggest that his value preferences are mere "prejudices," although here again it is quite impossible to say what he really means, for he suggests that we rely on the opinion of "experts" in arriving at our value preferences.[8] Perhaps

7. "Does Moral Philosophy Rest on a Mistake?" *Mind*, N. S., Vol. XXI, 1912; reprinted in *Ethical Theories*, ed. A. I. Melden (New York, 1955).
8. *Op. cit.*, p. 176.

some sense can be made out of the notion of arriving at a set of prejudices through the help of experts, but it is not easy. At any rate, it is surely an extraordinary use of language to call this moral judgment. If any sense can be made of the preferential view, the implication is of institutional determinism, a factual description, not a moral theory.

Thus it is evident how partial and improper description and definition of the plain facts of moral and political existence have resulted in a kind of moral impasse. The fact of institution has not been properly defined, but distorted as a fiction. Ignorance of this imposing area of fact has, in turn, led to a completely erroneous description of the individual, for in any morally or politically meaningful sense, institutions are the source of a substantial part of the factual content of individuals. The unique, isolable, subjective, arbitrary individual of ethical theory is an illegitimate fiction, contrary to fact. Until ethical speculation begins with acceptable definitions of manifest fact, it will have nothing of importance to say about values or moral discrimination; it will continue to chatter aimlessly about persuasive definitions and emotive judgments, about arbitrary preferences and subjective assertions.

Our concentrated attention upon the individual as a political fact has had good but limited results. It is perfectly plain that the ethicist is referring to *something*, to some characteristic of the individual; it is better that our political system takes account of this quality, even though it is erroneously described as moral capacity. However, the mistaken notion that certain factual content of the individual is the source of the value discrimination of a moral person implies the quite false assumption that the value discriminations of moral persons constitute the immediate data of political theory and process. The moral discriminations of persons who have the capacity to make such evaluations certainly constitute factual data for political concern, but it is most important to distinguish what is factual and what is evaluative; these two sources of influence on the political process are subject to quite different kinds of control since they are essentially different in kind. The assumption that one is dealing with a moral discrimination, when actually the datum in question is factual, is indicative of elementary error from which only misstatement of the problem can follow. To be sure, an individual exhibits preferences; more precisely, the individual is *disposed* toward certain kinds of action. To designate this *disposition* of the individual a moral discrimination or value-attitude is to use the terms "moral" and "value" so ambiguously that they lose meaning-reference. On the other hand, to assess the value discriminations of individuals as nothing more than the factual evidence of their institutional preferences is to ignore or distort a significant element of the political process. The individual in political context evidences certain characteristics which can be described only by reference to that context. Political context is the configuration or pattern of institutional structures of the particular polity.[9] The individual also evidences other capacities which, while they cannot be isolated from that context, enable him to assume an objective perspective toward that context.

The most pressing and critical task of political philosophy is that of informing us as to the nature and structure of institutions, since it is only on the basis of such factual information that we can expect to integrate individual and institutional facts into judgments about values in political structure. We should be prepared to find that within the terminology of our individualistic political philosophy there is hardly any term as ambiguous as "institution." It is used grandly and lamely, distributively and specifically; it is at once anything, everything, and nothing. Now there is a generally accepted method by which we set about describing fact, and it is in some such reasonable way that we must examine institutional structures. The individualistic description which ascribes will, purpose, and intelligence to a corporate organi-

9. Bentham came close to recognizing that "disposition" is institutional in origin (*The Limits of Jurisprudence Defined*), one of the suggestions for further development referred to above, p. 94 ff. So did Aristotle.

zation confuses the description and systematizing of fact by improper designation. Institutions have *institutional* characteristics; it indicates a dreadful paucity of language to name those facts "will" and "purpose." Nor is this descriptive ambiguity to be avoided simply by multiplication of the fundamental error. It will not do to describe an institution as a "group" or "association" or "collectivity" of individuals. Admittedly, it is hardly possible to think of an institution without persons; but it is just as impossible to conceive realistically (or politically) of individuals without institutions. Both individual and institution are essential and elementary *facts* of social and political existence. The institution has, as does the individual, a distinguishable factual existence, and this existence cannot be identified with the collective existences of the individuals who participate in the institution. There is factually something more to a corporation than the individual members of its board of directors; a university indicates a factual configuration which cannot be defined by a mere enumeration of its trustees, administration, faculty, and students.

Factual description is the proper function of the sciences, in political connotation primarily, but not exclusively, the social sciences. The concern here is limited, and no pretense can be made to competence in the wide range of expertness which must contribute to the clarification of the factual nature of institutions. There are, however, certain aspects of the relation of the individual and the institution in political structures that are a matter of immediate philosophical concern. This relationship must be understood if we are to exert control over, or effect changes in, the complexity of institutional structures which constitute any modern, industrial, technological state. In this respect, the significant characteristic of institutions is the fact that they are the sources of the *instruments* for individual action. There is literally nothing that the individual can *do* that does not involve the use of tools and materials which are provided him only through the institutional channels of his society. True, there is the realm of imagination where one can *not do* to his heart's content (although even here his concepts will be constructed within the definitive framework imposed by the institutions he knows) ; but while some may consider imagination to be the most significant of man's capacities, it is not a direct concern of political theory and politics. Even the artist must submit to the provision of materials by institutional channels if he endeavors to bring his imaginative construction into actual existence.

It is the function of an institution to provide instruments, and those instruments are what we mean, or ought to mean, by *property* objects. The attempt to define property solely in terms of private possession, rather than in terms of the useful instrument it properly is, represents one of the ambiguous concepts resulting from an improper reference of individualistic terminology. The institution is an organization of property objects which enables the individual to achieve purposes in action. The individual who thinks that his purposes and values are going to be achieved in action without adjustment to the nature and source of the instruments provided to him by institutions is courting disillusionment. His purposes will have a happier outcome if he understands institutions and adjusts his expectations to the available instruments of action. Institutions are, therefore, in this very real sense, restrictive upon the realizable purposes of individuals. There is no suggestion here that institutional determinism is the inescapable consequence of political organization. Intelligence, purpose, and will are factual characteristics of the individual, and it should be possible for individuals to effect changes in institutional structure and function; how they can effectively do so is perhaps the most important problem of political philosophy.

In the modern world there is no escape for the individual from the pervasive and encompassing restraint of the institutions of his political state, perhaps one of the most significant and drastic differences between all previous political theory and that which must make sense in our century. American thought, in particular, must have been strongly influenced by the conviction that man could indeed escape from institutional pressures which he did not approve and, with like-minded *emigrés*, set up institutions more to his liking and purpose. Certainly, the development of institutions in the United States during the eighteenth and nineteenth centuries was greatly influenced by such men, escapees from unsatisfactory political institutional configurations. This alternative to the discouragingly hard task of trying to change the institutions in which one finds himself enmeshed is no longer available to even the boldest and most courageous of men. Apart from the unpalatable and self-defeating alternatives of suicide or of blowing himself back into a communitarian isolationism, man cannot escape his institutions by fleeing from them. In fact, the alternatives in this respect which are available to man in the present world have become so restricted that he no longer has even the option of choosing to transport himself from one political configuration to a more satisfactory one; necessary and increasingly limited immigration allowances, walls, barbed wire, and mine fields operate in our world to remove almost completely for the individual the opportunity of escape from oppressive institutional configurations. The sole remaining alternatives are acceptance of the state in which one finds oneself, a resigned admission of the priority of the *ad hoc* or *de facto* over the *de jure,* or the assertion of one's moral capacity and dignity, however difficult or dangerous this may be, in an attempt to change the institutions which history and circumstances have imposed upon one.

Changing institutions is, however, an exceedingly difficult and slow process. Individuals as such can be influenced, even converted; in fact, their opinions sometimes seem to shift so rapidly that were there no stabilizing restraint on individual variabilities, the resultant fluctuations would be disastrous for any social or political organization. Stability is provided by institutions, which evidence in their nature a kind of *autonomy* of operation which absorbs the differences and shifts of

individual variance. It has apparently been a perplexing fact
of history to the philosophy of individualism that revolutions
and wars so often seem to have little influence on existing institutional structures, which somehow force men, even after
a period of destructive violence, back into their accustomed
channels and methods of action. The man who is ignorant of
the steadfast influence of institutions on his purposes and
actions may proclaim himself free, but he is in *fact* the unwitting victim of a determinism he does not even perceive.[10]

Let us very briefly consider the nature of this institutional
impact on the purposes and actions of individuals. In the first
place, we must admit that very few individuals will effect, as
individuals, any appreciable change in the institutional structure in which the accident of birth placed them. Further, it is
no depreciation of the courage or the genius of the hero in
history to remark that the success of the leader depends directly upon the *disposition* of those he leads. This disposition
reflects, through the individual, the stability and autonomy of
the institutions which constitute his culture; disposition is
therefore not susceptible to the kind of shift and variation
which characterizes opinion and even value judgment. The institution is for the individual the omnipresent influence, the
inexorable molder of individual actions and purposes to the
established modes of procedure, to the nature of the instruments provided by the institution to the individual. What
this constant and inescapable impact of the institution produces in the individual is not a rational, discriminating analysis of the situation of action, but rather an acceptance of the
provided instruments of action, with the accompanying adjustment or adaptation of purposes and values which may be
necessitated. The individual is *disposed* to accept these instruments and this mode of procedure because they are available,
because he has little or no alternative, and because some kind

10. Note the prophetic warning of Lincoln in his *First Inaugural Address:*
"Suppose you go to war, you cannot fight always; and when, after much loss on
both sides, and no gain on either, you cease fighting, the identical old questions
as to the terms of the intercourse are again upon you."

of action is necessary. As the artisan develops muscles and calluses from the use of his tools, so do all individuals develop inclinations and preferences from the historic use and influence of the institutions within which they act. Be his acceptance witless or wise, grudging or grateful, the individual finds himself disposed to act in certain ways because of the channels of action that are available to him. He has an inculcated disposition which is subrational, unavoidable, and extremely difficult to change or resist.

Now the important consideration for political theory is that this disposition of the individual is a *fact*, an elementary political fact. It is an intricate and complex fact, for in any but the most primitive of cultures the individual will be subject to a heterogeneous institutional configuration in which the disposition appropriate to one kind of action may be, and likely will be, different from that of other areas of his action. The disposition of an individual is not likely to be unitary unless he is an extraordinarily simple kind of individual; rather, it is to be expected that his preferences will vary according to the kind of action he envisages—that is, what institution serves his present purpose. However complex or however heterogeneous, this institutionally induced disposition is factual and subject to description and definition, even though such analysis be difficult and not promising of precise and exact formulation. If this manifestation of disposition by individuals is mistakenly assumed to be itself a value judgment, or even the reflection of a deliberative moral discrimination, then the problem of elementary political and legal order will be confused at its most fundamental level of analysis.

In its positive manifestation, disposition is not deliberative or discriminating; only in the negative instance of resistance on the part of the individual to an institutionally produced disposition does the individual become rationally deliberative. Moral judgment, on the other hand, must be deliberative and rational; it is, in fact, what the individual does if and when a disposition is questioned and examined. Perhaps the most serious problem to be faced by a moral person is the discovery of an institutionalized disposition in himself which is not consistent with his rational, deliberative moral judgment. Upon analysis of this painful situation, it immediately becomes evident that preachment and moral suasion do not resolve this social and political dilemma. Unless the institutional structure which produced the disposition is changed, the individual will find himself forced back into the very pattern of action which produced his disposition, regardless of the dictate or dissatisfaction of his value deliberation. Disposition, as inculcated by institutional structure, is a political fact, and it is not to be changed simply by giving it a value designation and declaring the fact "bad."

Consider, for example, the not at all unrealistic dilemma of a young person who has lived the eighteen years of his life in a community in which all activity is segregated. The segregation may be on the basis of color, race, religion, nationality, or caste. Whatever the kind of segregation, it is imposed by the institutional structure of the community, historic in origin and omnipresent in impact—through economics, religion, education, family, and politics. Suppose this person leaves the community of his origin and development, to go to college perhaps, or to travel. In different institutional circumstances, he observes, thinks, and arrives at a value discrimination, for whatever reason, that the segregation to which he has been accustomed is not justified. Such a determination will not be easy, for all of this person's disposition, concepts, and modes of action have been molded by those institutionally segregated patterns. However, the realization of such a moral discrimination through rational reflection is not impossible, nor is it at all unusual.

What happens, then, when this student or traveler returns to his home community, whether it be in the United States, India, South Africa, or the U.S.S.R.? In the short time of his absence, however revolutionary may have been his own personal moral experience, it is not likely that any revolutions have occurred in the institutions from which he departed two, three, or four years ago. If he is to live in this community, from pressure of circumstance or choice, his actions in every area of endeavor will be within those institutional patterns he now finds unsatisfactory. But act within them he must, for they are his only instruments of action. The dilemma faced by the individual in a conflict of moral judgment and political fact is not peculiar to our particular period of history, and short of the achievement of an ideal society, it will remain a persistent problem. Those who see this as a simple question of moral conviction, of individual dedication, are themselves either simple-minded or fanatically blind to political fact. The effort of our protagonist of equality, in his attempt to effect orderly change in the institutional structure he inherited, will be slow and often painful.

The accomplishment of change in political structure is not the simple process that individualistic representational theory has assumed it to be. Disposition to obedience is the product of a particular institutional configuration, and calculation of disposition can be reliably predicated only on an examination of that institutional configuration. It cannot be predicated on the value choices of individuals, since the law which controls or changes institutional procedures cannot in fact accomplish the achievement of values; it can only attempt to provide the instruments which might make possible the realization of individual purposes and values.

The management and control of institutional instruments in the political structure are the function of administration. Never before have the moral judgments of man so depended for their realization on the administration of the institutions through which alone those value aspirations can achieve any degree of factual reality. The prevailing myth of the eighteenth and nineteenth centuries, that a political society properly oriented to acceptable moral principles would, because of the efficacy or force of those principles, be self-administering in the achievement of those values, will not withstand the most superficial scrutiny of contemporary political organization. The expansion, the confusion, the inertia, the restraining influence (the potential power for control of all the instruments to man's actions), which are exhibited by administrative processes in all modern political structures, present a discouraging prognosis for moral and rational existence. Our lack of attention to this rapidly burgeoning area of the modern state, and our accompanying failure to accommodate it within our political philosophy, have made it possible for wide areas of administrative discretion to acquire power and authority without responsibility or accountability.[11]

In the modern state, the realization, even the sense, of an individual's moral judgments is immediately dependent upon the administration of the political fact of that state. If existing political fact circumvents or precludes the achievement of moral dignity and action, the individual has no recourse but to try to effect a change in the administration of that political fact. Hence, direction and control of the administrative processes of the state are requirements preliminary to the moral life of man. The philosophy of administration is a prerequisite concern of moral philosophy; the nature of the administrative function, its control, and the assessment of responsibility and accountability in the administration of political fact constitute an area of concern so significant that inattention to it can result only in moral apathy or impotence.

11. "The civil servant too often suffers from the optical illusion that the public is a herd of Gadarene swine. He sees politicians stampeded into unwise policies by the pressure of the public. . . . Public stampedes, to judge from the past, have always been caused by lack of information, or twisted information, not by a surfeit.

"In the last hundred years in Europe there have been repeated attempts to abolish arbitrary powers: of judges by codifying laws, of politicians by writing constitutions, of public officials by creating administrative courts. Arbitrary power has now been replaced by anonymous power, and anonymous power is the antonym of public administration" (Brian Chapman, *The Profession of Government* [London, 1959], p. 322).

[CHAPTER VII]

THE ADMINISTRATION OF
POLITICAL FACT

In our society experts are good servants but indifferent masters.[1]

THE complexity of contemporary social structure makes the control and change of administrative machinery a most formidable task, one which will not be resolved by inattention and ought not to be sacrificed to accident or expediency. The scope and size of the machinery present a challenge; man will either control that machinery to his ultimate purposes or forego the possibility of meaningful moral life. The increasing absorption of all the facts of existence by the machinery of organization is a perplexity of modern life, but the ironic suggestion of Samuel Butler in *Erewhon* that we relegate machines to a museum and return to a simpler life is hardly a real alternative. Machinery, administrative or any other kind, is not essentially or intrinsically bad.

> Ends come into existence then through the *adequate embodiment of purpose in forms objectified in action,* and this statement is the whole philosophy of the practical life and the ground principle of administration. . . . The growth of ends and their integration into systems and orders directly implicates the multiplication of machinery, so that mechanization of life is not necessarily an evil. . . . What we lament about machinery is then not the number or the adequacy or serviceableness of machines taken as isolated tools, but the disorder of their

1. Sir Noel F. Hall, *The Making of Higher Executives,* (New York, 1958), p. 99.

relations and the fact that they as a whole have no assign-able meaning.[2]

The assignment of meaning to the administrative machin-ery of the state, if it is to be anything more than the acceptance of senseless self-perpetuation of the mechanism, must involve some assessment of purpose. Administration must exhibit some purpose other than its own maintenance or the verifica-tion of Parkinson's law. We have seen that political authority cannot be justified as deriving from a particular moral code or system, and the question is whether this qualification applies to the administrative as well as to the political func-tion of the state. When we speak of the "purpose" of admin-istration, we are not making reference to a specific, identifiable moral purpose; rather, such usage seems to be in the same sense in which, in ordinary discourse, we refer to the "pur-pose" of a desk or a hammer or traffic regulations. It would probably be more precise to use the term "function" instead of "purpose" in this connection, since the duality of the word "purpose" tends to drag us back into the very confusion we are trying to avoid.[3] The somewhat random usage of ordinary language is resistant to precise distinctions, and we shall un-doubtedly continue to talk about "good" administration and "bad" administrators. However, the distinction we are trying to maintain here is essential to meaningful political discourse, and we must try, however beset by the usages of common dic-tion, to recognize that the evaluation of political processes is not to be accomplished on the basis of whether or not they have conformed to a particular set of moral rules or principles.

At this point it may be useful to summarize the observations which have indicated the critical importance of the adminis-tration of political fact to the possibility of any effectiveness

---

2. E. Jordan, *Theory of Legislation* (Chicago, 1952), pp. 392-393.

3. It is an almost irresistible temptation to advance from the description of a "good" desk or hammer as one that fulfils its "purpose" to the analogical definition of a "good" statesman as one who fulfils his "purpose." The ap-parently self-evident purposes of the desk and hammer thereby become the unwarranted ground for assuming that the purpose of the statesman is equally self-evident.

of moral judgment. The emphasis on the proper administration of political fact as a prerequisite to the sensible statement and eventual realization of individual moral judgments is in some respects a rather radical departure from our traditional framework of moral reference. Yet, if moral judgment is to make any sense at all within the context of political fact, which is the context in which we live and act, it must take cognizance of the potential for recognition and realization, or denial and defeat, of the moral purposes of men by the administrative function in modern society. The control of the effective instruments of the modern state is in the hands of the administrators of those instruments, and therefore the control of administration will mark the availability of means for the moral achievement of man.

We could, of course, at this point introduce the question whether it is the end or purpose of existence that man *should* be provided an opportunity to achieve moral status and dignity. The query might almost place us in the predicament of Bentham with respect to government: we make an assumption, and if denied it, we are at a loss to try to justify it. There is, however, no real question at issue, for all of the political and moral theories we have examined hold as their ultimate end the achievement of moral stature for men. These diverse theories suggest the attainment of that end by a conflicting divergence of means to the end. It is precisely on this consideration—and not on whether our ultimate purpose is the moral status of man—that we find ourselves in disagreement. There is a logical impasse involved in any view which suggests that the moral realization of man can be achieved by the imposition of an authoritative legislation of a moral code, from whatever source it claims origin.

Our discussion of the relation of political authority and morals has indicated that the use of that authority to impose a moral view is to defeat the very purpose of moral judgment. The police state, as an exhibition of authority through sheer force, not only fails to show any justification for the exercise of that authority, but also makes impossible the achievement of moral judgment in any meaningful sense. On the other hand, a government which offers a legal justification for its authority can rest its claim for justification on the ground that its authority derives from a disposition to obedience on the part of those to whom the law is directed. This nature of the claim of legal justification has been asserted throughout the history of political thought, by Aristotle, Hobbes, Bentham, and others. On this view, the ultimate sovereignty of the legal state derives more or less directly from that disposition, and such a state may thus make a claim of *de jure* sovereignty. An important consideration of this analysis is that the claim of justification for the legal state is not by reference to moral principles, but on the basis of political fact.

The term "disposition" has a factual reference, although it is admittedly complex and difficult of specification. However loosely we may use the terms "democracy" and "representative," there is implicit in the reference to disposition as the justification for political authority a factual assertion of democratic or representative method, although in the modern state it bears little resemblance to the simple, face-to-face relations of a town-meeting kind of political structure. The individualistic conceptual framework and language of our political philosophy have made it difficult to clarify the fact of disposition in the context of the modern state, and our persistence in identifying disposition with moral sentiment confuses an issue which is a challenge to analysis even when free of confusion. The mistaken identification of political authority with moral principle has resulted in the erroneous notion that a particular legal system derives its authority from a particular moral system; the effect of this misconception is to make any communication or adjustment between different legal and political systems difficult and unsatisfactory.

The distinguishing feature of *legal* systems of political authority has been that they have *not* been grounded in a particular moral system, but on the contrary their aim has been to maintain a political structure which will accommodate the maximum possible exercise of moral judgment by the individuals within that structure. The aim of such a political order, to achieve the highest possible degree of rational judgment for its members, has been deplorably confused by a development of non-rational and antirational moral theories in British and American philosophy. If moral judgment is described as the mere assertion of an attitude, a preference, or a disposition, man is indeed not a rational being, but a system of psychological states of mind which have been institutionally produced.

The disposition of an individual will reflect the complex of institutional structures in which he exists and acts. A particular configuration of institutional structures is what we ought to mean when we refer to a *state*. The citizens of any particular state have acquired dispositions as the result of having acted within the institutions of that state because those institutions have provided them with the only instruments for action that are available to them. These dispositions are not rational or deliberative; it is when rational deliberation brings into question the action which results from such dispositions that the problems of moral judgment arise.

One principle of justification for the authority of law and the state is that it is consistent with the dispositions to obedience of those to whom it is addressed. This criterion is not subjectivistic, as we have seen. Rather, when we clarify what we mean by *dispositions,* it is apparent that such a justification of legal authority is a recognition of the fundamental institutional structure of the state, and a recognition of the necessity for order and continuity in that configuration. The rule of *stare decisis,* despite frequent ridicule, is an essential requirement of legal procedure. Authority which can justify its legality will thus to the best of its ability maintain orderly relations among the manifold institutional instruments available to men in the state.

What has been described is the *factual* justification of legal authority, and in this sense it is logically prior to any other claim of justification. It is on the question as to whether or not this factual claim of legal authority is a *sufficient* justification that a sharp and irreducible difference in political philosophies develops. The value assertion that the end of man is rational, deliberative, moral judgment—and not mere acceptance of institutional directions and duties, however legally ordered—requires that legal authority also be responsive to this ultimate end of moral judgment. We may assert this recognition to be the distinguishing feature of democratic political philosophy, thereby putting the much abused concept of *democracy* in a meaningful context. On the basis of this observation, democracy must be understood as a political philosophy which differs from others in a sense which is more fundamental and profound than mere difference in forms or procedures.[4]

The requirement that legal and political authority recognize that the ultimate end of the state is the achievement by man of the capacity and conditions of moral judgment does not in any way whatever suggest that that authority derives its sanction from any moral judgment or set of moral judgments. Men may and do utilize the instruments of education for unselfish and humane ends, for avarice and greed, for egoistic prestige, for scholarly satisfaction, and for numerous other ends based on personal judgment. The administration of educational institutions cannot properly be directed or controlled by any one or all of these moral judgments. It is on the subject of the administration of institutions that our own political tradition has been most unclear. In the analysis of any set of relationships, it is most important (as Kant observed) that the order of the relationship be properly recognized. Unless we are clear about the order of relation between disposition and

4. As with such terms as "sovereignty," "command," "morals," and "authority," democracy as a concept has been so ill-treated that surely we sometimes are embarrassed to use the term. There is no reason why it cannot be used as a definable and meaningful concept which should not be abandoned because it has been loosely handled.

authority, and between authority and moral judgment, the question of what we are trying to do in the exercise of political authority will be inextricably confused.

The disposition which is institutionally induced is not moral choice; since political authority which can claim legal justification (i.e., which is not the authority of sheer force) derives from disposition, legal authority is not derivable from moral choice. Sincere proponents of democratic processes still court disillusionment when they assume that the establishment of a system of legal and political authority is simply a matter of the moral choice of the individuals involved. History is replete with examples of the futility of attempting to transpose or impose democratic procedures on a social structure in which the institutional configuration has not been of a kind to produce or induce in its citizens a disposition to the obedience (and appreciation) of the law which is necessary to the maintenance of a democratic philosophy. The preliminary *sine qua non* of the realization of the democratic end of the moral dignity of man is the establishment of an institutional structure which will provide the factual conditions for that moral status.

The representative and parliamentarian processes of democratic government are procedures designed to facilitate the expression of individual value discriminations and aspirations. The democratic system of government is responsive to the demand of individuals that changes in the institutional structure, however gradual, be accomplished in order to make available to men a wider and more satisfactory range of value realization. Progressively, democratic governments have accomplished such changes in economic institutions, in education, in health, in recreation, and in other areas which in times past had hardly come under the scrutiny of political philosophy. This philosophy of government has indeed tried, with some considerable success, to enlarge the possibilities of man's moral judgment and realization.

The entire history of social improvement has been a series

of transitions, by which one custom or institution after another, from being a supposed primary necessity of social existence, has passed into the rank of a universally stigmatised injustice and tyranny. So it has been with the distinctions of slaves and freemen, nobles and serfs, patricians and plebeians; and so it will be, and in part already is, with the aristocracies of colour, race, and sex.[5]

The unhappy and unpalatable observation which must be made about contemporary democratic philosophy is that all of its sincere efforts in representation, parliamentarian legislation, and respect for the individual can, in the modern world, be negated by the administration of an institutional structure which has become complex and bureaucratic beyond the belief of the eighteenth-century philosophers who proclaimed the dignity of man. The administration of institutions, unless controlled, promises man the final indignity of moral sterility.

Although the problem of maintaining a democratic political structure which will facilitate the maximum achievement of individual moral judgments seems more complex and difficult in modern society than ever before, it is by no means a new problem. Political philosophers from Plato to the present have persistently tried to resolve the question of value achievement by the proclamation or the construction of a homogeneous value structure in the state. That there must be some homogeneity in the ordered relationships of the institutions and values in a state we have already observed; the state is indeed the structure which maintains such ordered relations within a particular set of institutions. However, this requirement is quite different from that which imposes homogeneity upon the values which are to be achieved ultimately by the moral judgment of individuals. The establishment of a mandated priority in the values which individuals will be permitted to achieve is a negation of the most fundamental premise of democratic philosophy.

The achievement of political order by the enforcement of a

5. J. S. Mill, *Utilitarianism* (London, 1863), chap. v.

monolithic value hierarchy has always been a very tempting alternative to the heterogeneity of a democratic polity, which must accommodate the widest possible range of values. The problem of authority in the democratic state is clearly much more difficult of analysis and resolution than it is in the state which deliberately makes all value realization dependent upon the prior satisfaction of the single value enunciated by the leader or leaders. So Plato restricted value discrimination to the intellectual elite; Campanella would achieve order by the political use of religion and the confessional in a form of brainwashing for the service of the state; the complications of modern society forced H. G. Wells to suggest control by a technologically trained and dedicated administrative elite; the horror of George Orwell's *Nineteen Eighty-Four* is that such reduction of the moral judgment of the individual to a minimum approaching extinction appears more nearly possible in our technological, centralized society than ever before in our history. The past and present provide us with recurring examples of states which have attempted to establish authority by the method of total value reduction. The democratic state is a multi-valued state, by definition, and this prescription must control the policy of the administration of the democratic state as well as the policy of its representational processes.

[11]

Democracy is representative *and* administrative government. It asserts that the value discriminations of individuals must be expressed and communicated through the representative process. However, it has been argued here that the law which formalizes and promulgates the system of order which will make possible the realization of those values cannot itself have authority unless the institutional organization of the state has produced an appropriate disposition to obedience. The organization and management of institutions are the function of administration, and the actual realization of policies determined by legislation depends directly upon the effectiveness of the administrative function. However, these two functions of the democratic political process are different in kind; they are separate and distinguishable, and the principles and procedures which are appropriate to each must be clarified in any philosophy adequate to the modern democratic state. If their distinguishable functions are not cognized, the potential conflict of the two areas of government action will defeat the very purpose of democratic philosophy.

The function of representative legislation is policy-making, directed by the multiple value discriminations of the individuals in the state. The function of administration is not policy-making, but policy-realization. The necessary bureaucracy of the state is, in a democracy, subordinate to the legislative function, in that administration is obliged to realize, to the degree that is possible, the policy dictated by legislative action; the legislator, in turn, is obliged to respect the mandate of the electorate. If this relationship of the accountability of the administrative function to the legislative is not maintained, the essential purpose of democratic representative government will be short-circuited.

The clarification of the relation of these two areas of governmental enterprise is not easy, and considerably more philosophical attention must be directed to the problem than it has received in the recent past. It was with the greatest reluctance that we were finally forced to the recognition that the principles which are reasonably successful in the area of representational legislation are inappropriate and indeed calamitous in the area of administration. Our devastating war between the Northern and Southern states showed starkly and horribly the result of applying principles appropriate to democratic representation to the area of military administration, where competence and expertness are needed. The representational election of military officers is a bid for disaster, and so it is in any other area of administrative control. The necessary principle that administration must be accountable for the realization of legislative policy does not therefore imply that the administrator is in any sense subject to the principles, rules, procedures, or criteria which govern the representative legislative system. The administrator is not a legislator; the legislator must not try to be an administrator. We must attempt to define and delimit these supplementary functions, both of which are essential to the realization of policy and stability in democratic government.

The legislative function will be improperly performed unless attention is given to all three of the following factors:

1. Law must formulate policy as directed by the representative process.

2. The effectiveness of the administration of law will depend on the disposition to obedience of those to whom the law is directed *and* on the efficiency of the administrative process.

3. The realization of policy by administration in the control and management of the institutional structure of the state will determine the dispositions of individuals on which future law (and ultimately the authority of the state) must depend.

The sovereignty and authority of the state, therefore, depend directly upon the administrative management of the institutional structure of the state. Administration today will effect and determine disposition tomorrow, and in any potential conflict between values or policy and disposition, policy will have to be sacrificed to the enforceability of law. This important, and possibly critical, influence of administration must be clearly recognized and contained, or the values for which alone democratic government exists could be rendered impossible by administrative control of institutions.

The relation of the legislative and administrative functions in democracy is not simply a distinction of two parallel governmental activities; it involves rather a reconsideration of democratic political philosophy in terms of the vast administrative machinery of the modern state. The boundaries of administrative discretion must be specified in any political philosophy adequate to the contemporary state, and such specification cannot be accomplished through the dictates of temporary expediency, but only on the basis of an application of the principles of the political philosophy of the state, democratic or not. The problem of communication between the policy-making organ and the administrative bureaucracy is not, in other words, peculiar to a democratic or representational political structure. However difficult the problem may appear in our own government, however haphazard the relation may at times seem to be, there are perhaps both consolation and promise in the observation that modern technological states whose policies are determined in non-democratic fashion are beset by just the same question of how to prevent the miscarriage of policy by administration. In fact, the course of events has indicated clearly that states with a political organization such as that of the U.S.S.R. face even greater difficulties in this respect than do democratic states. Effective communication is reciprocal communication, and a political method which is dependent on a one-way dispensation of authority by a hierarchical monopoly of power responsible only to itself is ill-suited to the needs of communication today. It has been demonstrated that there are limits to the effectiveness of edicts of authority to peasants; how much more apparent it is that communication by edict will be even less effective in areas of scientific, skilled, and technical competence. It is a vivid exhibition of authority to demean, punish, even execute an administrator for failure to achieve unrealistic or absurd policy goals, but it is certainly questionable whether this method is productive of efficiency in administration.

The task of administration is to effect legislated policy and thereby to make possible the realization of values. The determination of values by administration is contradictory to democratic principles. However, there are in most instances alternate methods available by which the instruments appropriate to individual purposes may be provided. The determination of the most effective method for realization of the policy-end is the proper discretion of administration; this is a factual rather than a value discrimination, and establishes the essential role of the expert in the administrative process. The function of the expert in administration emphasizes the necessity for continued and effective communication between the processes of policy formation and policy realization; only on the basis of such an exchange can each be adequately informed in the discharge of its function. Sporadic and unsystematic efforts to establish such communication by *ad hoc* legislative investigation of administrative agencies serve poorly this essential requirement of legislative-administrative liaison. Such procedure is generally invoked only after the legislative-administrative relation has approached a point of near-rupture; however well-intentioned the participants, break-down in communication characteristically induces short tempers, personal badgering or vilification, and distortion or concealment of the facts which ought to be a subject of discussion rather than of controversy. In our political system, control over policy must be maintained by the legislative; it is simply regrettable that we have given little attention to the development of a more efficient and just procedure for exercising that control.

It seems fair to suggest that the legislators in our political system are more sensitive to this problem than are our administrators.[6] The nature of administration, whether democratic or not, is such as to induce in a vested bureaucracy a sense of well-being proportionate to its relief from accountability and responsibility. Any suggestion that the administrator should himself be accountable, as is the legislator in our system, is likely to evoke protests of interference and political sabotage

6. One exception is former Federal Trade Commissioner Lowell Mason, *The Language of Dissent* (Cleveland, 1959). See also the reports of the Subcommittee on Administrative Practice and Procedure, Senate Judiciary Committee; the chairman of the subcommittee is Senator Henry Jackson.

of the "administration." Investigations of administrative agencies may on occasion be used for political purposes, but to suggest that legislative query about administrative action and responsibility is improper is to mistake a most fundamental and essential principle of democratic philosophy. However imperfect at times, control of policy by a legislative body continually responsible to its electorate is in *every* respect preferable to control of policy by a bureaucracy responsible to nothing but its own perpetuation.

It was of the greatest significance for the future development of the United States that those who were responsible for its first organization were so perceptive about the relation of legislation, administration, and the function of the executive. (George Washington ought more properly to be revered as the father of the country for his administrative genius than for his passing military prowess.[7]) It is doubtful that the history of politics exhibits another instance in which such a concentration of ability, intelligence, and integrity was directed to the discussion of an emerging political structure. Seen in this light, as concerned with the establishment of effective administrative procedure, the Federalists may be less harshly judged for their insistence on strong executive power. They did not seek power irresponsible and unaccountable to democratic processes; they recognized the necessity of control over administration, and in their philosophy this was the task of the executive office.

The subsequent decline, during the nineteenth century, of attention to, and understanding of, the necessity for administrative control and regulation cannot be charged entirely to mediocrity, cupidity, and the vagaries of democratic politics, although all of these were contributing elements in the exploitation of civil service and the rampant irresponsibility of administration. More important for our purposes here is the observation that the political philosophy of our eighteenth-

7. See the fine definitive work of Leonard D. White, *The Federalists: A Study in Administrative History* (New York, 1948), and the successive volumes of this history.

century democracy, for all its cognizance of the importance of administration, was inappropriate to the kind of state that had developed by the middle of the nineteenth century. What Washington could and did effect in control of administration, Lincoln could not achieve; integrity, courage, and intelligence were baffled by complexity.

As we face the latter half of the twentieth century, the eighteenth-century philosophy which defined the office of executive as a liaison between legislative and administrative branches—the custodian of responsibility—is so unrealistic that the persistence of the model in the face of the facts of modern society is an increasing menace to democratic government. The executive of a modern state can perform that function of liaison only by assuming the powers and prerogatives of a dictator or quasi-dictator. It is this significant development of twentieth-century politics which the democratic state must avoid.[8] The problem is not a new one; Alexis de Tocqueville described it in 1835. However, the physical and geographical circumstances which permitted survival despite administrative ineptitude do not exist today, and this is equally as true of industrial and business enterprise as of governmental organization. Efficiency and accountability in administration are today the most critical internal problem of the democratic state—more fundamental than production increase, taxes, even more consequential than civil rights. The agencies of administration now control all the instruments which are useful and necessary to the action and purposes of individuals. Never in history has the achievement of the moral purpose and stature of the individual been so directly and immediately dependent on the administrators of his society; his moral future depends on their responsibility.

All that is being said here is so obviously a matter of observa-

8. As an instance of the acceptance of the dictator-administrator resolution, see the work of presidential adviser Col. Edward M. House, *Philip Dru: Administrator; A Story of Tomorrow, 1920-1935* (New York, 1912). Administrator Dru is a young West Point graduate who leads a revolution in 1920, rules as a dictator (mildly, of course) for fifteen years, and then happily and unrealistically retires voluntarily to Europe.

tion that expression of it so emphatically can be justified only on the grounds of moral survival. The assessment of administrative responsibility can no longer be defined as merely a problem of organization or structure. Yet, despite the obvious and urgent need, there seems to be a strange apathy and reluctance to do anything about it. Little or no attention is paid to the infrequent and relatively mild suggestions that the complex and technical administrative agencies of government should not be directed and operated by untrained, unskilled, temporary, electioneering, and on the whole non-responsible appointees. Is it absurd to be alarmed when heads of vital administrative bureaus admit that they cannot discern or assign accountability in their own departments? Is it remarkable to argue that administrators should be trained? Is it preposterous to suggest that the realization of democratic philosophy today necessitates the establishment and maintenance of liaison between the legislative and the administrative? It is mandatory that we have a permanent, instructed, and informed branch of government organization which is assigned the task of inspecting, analyzing, assessing, and reporting on the organization and performance of the administrative agencies which are purportedly our civil servants. Such a branch of government would be an essential supplement to the legislative function, to which it would be responsible. Should it be suggested that this proposal augurs only a further expansion of burgeoning bureaucracy, the reply must be: quite the contrary. Some such systematic survey of the administrative processes is the only hopeful solution of the creeping paralysis of proliferation, the only way by which can be forestalled the believably predictable acme of administrative redundancy— the foreseeable future in which the "administration" of the Department of Agriculture outnumbers the farmer population.

The change in governmental structure which such a proposal envisages is not a matter for casual debate or amateur tinkering. It would be outside the bounds of this discussion to propose specific and detailed forms of procedure; sufficient to our task is the suggestion that we recognize the problem, give thought to it, and move toward the organization of a democratic polity which will give to modern man promise of moral realization.

[III]

At the conclusion of this theoretical—and in some respects rather negative—appraisal of administration in modern society, it is appropriate to recognize a major practical and positive contribution to the clarification of a philosophy of administration. The organization and operation of Administrative Staff Colleges in England and the Commonwealth countries may well prove to be one of the most significant political developments of our time. The background of this extensive, concentrated, and systematic approach to administration was twofold. In the first place, the long concern with bureaucratic organization and career administration produced a wide range of thinking in Great Britain which responded actively to some facts about administration made abundantly clear by the urgent pressures of World War II:

1. The critical importance of the administrator in the provision of instruments for action.

2. The necessity for trained and expert administrators in modern society, not products of political or haphazard selection.

3. The recognition that the requisite expertness of the administrator is not so specialized that his ability is not transferable.

4. Finally, and of the greatest importance, the observation that in respect to a dominant policy of public purpose, supposed conflicts in administration are often minimal and almost always amenable to adjustment.

The second controlling factor was the impact of a philosophy of administration appropriate to the structure of the modern state. In this climate of opinion and purpose the experiment of the Administrative Staff College at Henley-on-Thames was begun.[9] Concern with the structure and function of administration in the entire body politic distinguished the Administrative Staff College at the very outset from management institutes and the in-service schools of civil and military agencies. This purposive direction according to a theory of administration which is appropriate to the context of the contemporary democratic state has resulted in the remarkable continuity and expansion of the Administrative Staff College idea. That idea has spread to Australia, India, Jugoslavia, New Zealand, Pakistan, the Philippines, and the West Indies, either in the creation of Staff Colleges similar to that at Henley or in programs influenced by that experience. Staff members from Henley continue to serve throughout the world in advisory capacities; in addition, over three hundred "graduates" of the course at Henley have gone back to some fifty countries outside the United Kingdom.[10]

In the work cited above, Hall quotes with approval the remark of T. N. Whitehead that "the business man's functions come near to disintegrating the society whose economic future he is providing for."[11] A basic principle of the political philosophy which was directive in the organization and operation of the College derives from the "fear that the fragmenta-

9. Sir Noel Frederick Hall was the Principal of the Administrative Staff College at Henley from its inception in 1945 (first session 1948) until 1961, when he returned to academic life as Principal of his alma mater, Brasenose College, Oxford. Before World War II, he was Professor of Political Economy, University College, University of London; during the war, he was Minister Plenipotentiary in charge of the War Trade Department at the British Embassy in Washington.

To him must be credited the discernment, and incorporation into the program of the College, of that philosophy of administration which is an essential and unique ingredient of its success. See his *The Making of Higher Executives: The Modern Challenge* (New York, 1958).

10. The philosophy of this Staff College idea is on the whole consistent with that expressed above in this chapter. My own thinking was indeed influenced by observation of the Staff College in operation when I was accorded the status of Staff Observer during session 38 (1960) at Henley.

11. *Leadership in a Free Society* (Cambridge, Mass., 1936), p. 80.

tion of tasks which technical efficiency requires may fragment the structure of society itself and thus render abortive in terms of human and social values the very advances in technical efficiency which require a greater and still greater division of labor."[12] Selective admission of the sixty-six or so participants in each session of twelve weeks maintains an institutional balance of representatives of business, industry, finance, civil service, national and local agencies, and the military services. It is interesting to note that recently for the first time trade unions also have nominated candidates for the College.

All of the various aspects of the College organization are designed to portray the administrative function as a potentially cohesive rather than a disruptive element in modern society. The aim is to induce in the administrator, whatever may be his area of institutional operation, a sense of responsibility transcending specialized, individual, or occupational interests. The requirement of residence for all participants, the total dedication of the entire staff, the relative isolation (without business or extracurricular distractions), and the method of selection all combine to produce in the relatively short time of twelve weeks a homogeneity of relationship, discussion, and exchange of ideas that is both novel and effective. As expressed by Hall:

> The method should in each case give opportunities to those who come to impart to others the benefits of their own experience, and to enable them to make comparisons between their experience and that of others. For the object of such courses is to insure that the future practical experience of participants will be more valuable to them because it will go into their minds with some comparative evaluation of it already made.[13]

It would not be appropriate to discuss here in detail the organization of the College, but the manner in which the purpose of the program is achieved may be briefly indicated.[14]

12. Hall, *op. cit.*, p. 8.
13. *Ibid.*, p. 94.
14. For a description of the mechanics and procedures of the College program, see Glenn Negley, "The British Administrative Staff College—Training for Executive Responsibility," *Personnel Administration*, XXV, No. 1 (1962), 35-42.

For instance, the first consideration in the course of studies is that of comparative administrative structures, and in this early stage there begins to appear more similiarity in the administrative organization of disparate enterprises than their representatives had assumed. The civil servant in a bureaucratic hierarchy finds it easier than he would ever have expected to sympathize with the problems of a business administrator who is accountable to his board of directors. The periodic reports that are presented by the discussion groups reflect an increasing understanding not only of the significance of the administrative function in social policy, but also of a recognition of the responsibility which this imposes upon the administrator at all levels of private and public activity. The report of one such discussion group is typical:

> As we have accepted that the common interest lies in the balance between social stability and the accumulation of wealth, it is fair to say that cooperation between government and industry is more important than ever before and that this importance is growing. It is essential that the senior people in government and industry are well informed in all relevant fields and can make correct assessments of the total picture.

This group represented a cross-section of finance, industry, business, civil service, and government.

The negative principle which is exposed in this approach to the administrative problem is clear: the requirements imposed by any philosophy of administration adequate to the modern state will be served poorly, if at all, by programs conducted by and within the administrative organization they are intended to serve. Such introverted activities may possibly communicate routine procedures of operations; more likely they will activate autonomy, increase insularity, and on the whole defeat the very purpose of increasing responsibility at all levels of administration. In fact, it is difficult to escape the observation that "within-bureau" programs are likely to convince the administrator that he will be well-advised to avoid responsibility whenever possible, not to suggest changes, and above all not to have "ideas."

The actual effect which the philosophy of the Administrative Staff College has had on individuals and institutions can hardly be assessed. However, it can be observed that in seventeen years some six hundred industries, businesses, banks, agencies, and bureaus have sent men to the College—at the expense of twelve weeks' loss of their services, in addition to the cost of tuition, residence, and travel. It would be unrealistic to suggest that these various enterprises are motivated simply by public interest; on the other hand, common sense dictates recognition of the fact that the directors of these manifold areas of administration are cognizant of their relation to political authority and public policy.

If this be true, then indeed some progress can be discerned in the communication of administrative responsibility. The realization of the purposes of democratic states is, in the modern world, immediately dependent on the maintenance of proper relations between the political and all administrative functions. Corporate activity can no longer be countenanced as the wilful and capricious manipulation of individual entrepreneurs. In respect to this problem of modern social and political organization, we might well attend to Bentham's principle of "utility." Preachments that the administrator should be moral and righteous in the discharge of his responsibilities are altogether less convincing than the straightforward factual observation that administration functions properly to serve the ends and purposes of public policy, whether determined democratically or otherwise. Administration which does not perform this function can be expected to "administrate" itself into chaos. Any effort, therefore, which aims to impress upon the administrator this elementary fact of contemporary political organization is of the greatest significance, for upon its success depends the moral status of all men.

INDEX